TEACHING
FOR
INQUIRY
Engaging the Learner Within

Ruth V. Small
Marilyn P. Arnone
Barbara K. Stripling
Pam Berger

Neal-Schuman Publishers, Inc.

New York   London

> ▶ Companion Website

Don't miss this book's companion website:

To access additional lessons, units, guides, bibliographies, strategies, and other library learning tools, go to:

http://teachingforinquiry.net

Published by Neal-Schuman Publishers, Inc.
100 William St., Suite 2004
New York, NY 10038
http://www.neal-schuman.com

Cover design by Marguerite Chadwick-Juner.

Printed and bound in the United States of America.

The paper used in this publication meets the minimum requirements of American National Standard for Information Sciences—Permanence of Paper for Printed Library Materials, ANSI Z39.48-1992.

Library of Congress Cataloging-in-Publication Data

Teaching for inquiry : engaging the learner within / Ruth V. Small ... [et al.].
    p. cm.
  Includes bibliographical references and index.
  ISBN 978-1-55570-755-2 (alk. paper)
  1. Information literacy—Study and teaching (Elementary) 2. Information literacy—Study and teaching (Secondary) 3. Inquiry-based learning. 4. School librarian participation in curriculum planning. 5. Library orientation for school children. 6. Research—Methodology—Study and teaching (Elementary) 7. Research—Methodology—Study and teaching (Secondary) I. Small, Ruth V.

ZA3075.T423 2012
028.7'071—dc23
                                                              2011033983

Contents

Chapter 6. Bringing It All Together   123

List of Illustrations

Figures

Tables

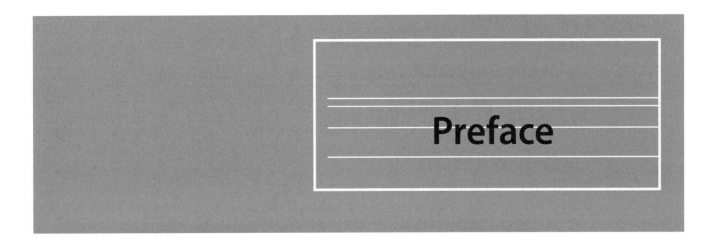

Preface

We begin *Teaching for Inquiry: Engaging the Learner Within* with two contrasting scenarios of what it might have been like for school librarians in the 1960s and the 1980s, and then compare their roles and responsibilities with a scenario from today's twenty-first-century school librarian. What we have learned about human learning and the evolution of technology over the past 50 years has dramatically changed what school librarians do and how they do it.

SCENARIO #1: 1965

It is 1965 and Deborah Jones is the school librarian at Main Street Elementary School in Collegetown, New York. Mrs. Jones has worked hard to make sure her collection of books and audiovisual materials is organized, up-to-date, and accessible through the card catalog. Today, she is spending most of the day preparing bibliographies and lists of new books for teachers. Four classes are scheduled to come to the library to exchange their library books. Later in the day, Deborah will visit two of the second grade classrooms with her book cart to deliver book talks on some of the new books. While having lunch in the teachers' room, Deborah is asked by John Bailey, the fourth grade teacher, if she could provide some suggestions of library materials that might help his students with their social studies research reports (each student has been assigned to submit a written report on one of the 50 states). Deborah returns to the library and begins putting together a bibliography and a lesson plan to teach John's students about how to use the encyclopedia in anticipation of their visits to the library to find information for their reports. She has a new filmstrip on "How to Use the Encyclopedia" that she plans to show them as part of her lesson.

SCENARIO #2: 1985

It is 1985. Glenn Cooper is the school library media specialist at Main Street Elementary School in Collegetown, New York. Mr. Cooper has worked hard to make sure his OPAC is kept up-to-date and that his library and information skills program reaches every child in the school during scheduled class visits to the library. One day last week after school, Glenn visited all of the fifth grade teachers in their classrooms about the social studies unit they are currently teaching and the culminating research report they have assigned to students, so that he could plan and implement information skills lessons to help prepare the students to do this assignment. Today, he is spending most of the morning working with the fifth grade students to help them apply their information skills to complete a social studies report on one of the 50 states. Later in the day, he will visit each of the second grade classrooms with his book cart to show the students and teachers some of the new books, magazines, audiocassettes, and videotapes that are now available in the library. Just before the day ends, two third grade girls come to the library to ask Mr. Cooper if he can help them find some more fantasy books like those they had just read. He shows them how to use the OPAC to find books by the same authors or books in the same genre. On his desktop computer, Glenn types a list of possible books he might order for them and sends it to the central library office.

Roles and Responsibilities of School Librarians

In 1965, Deborah Jones' role as a school librarian was mainly focused on building and maintaining a collection of books and audiovisual materials for use by teachers and students. While these materials may be integral to students' completion of classroom assignments and projects or were intended to support reading development and foster a leisure-time reading habit, this more passive role leaves Deborah on the fringe of the teaching-learning process. This disconnected role becomes even more defined when Mrs. Jones teaches students to use research materials out of context, removed from classroom learning activities and assignments.

Just 20 years later, by 1985, the librarian's role had shifted significantly, as a result of (1) an emphasis of pre-service preparation programs on the increasing teaching responsibilities of school librarians, (2) the shift from a focus on books and other information "packaged" to the information itself and how to use, evaluate, manage, organize, and present it, and (3) the promise of distributed, networked technology that was looming on the horizon. However, we see that Glenn is still not an integral player in the instructional planning process, teaching mostly scheduled classes and teaching information skills as a resource rather than as a process.

Recognizing that the responsibilities of the school librarian have changed and evolved dramatically over the past 50 years, librarians are now playing an increasingly important and more active role in the educational mission of their schools. Once mainly consisting of being solely an information provider of needed print, then audiovisual, materials to teachers and students, the role of school librarians has evolved and expanded to being more active partners in the total educational process.

With the dawn of the twenty-first century and the introduction of the newest AASL standards in 2007, today's school librarian now plays an integral role in the teaching and learning process. The twenty-first-century school library professional can now describe that role as:

1. serving as an essential contributing member of school and/or district curriculum and technology committees and teacher planning teams;

2. introducing teachers and students to the newest learning technologies and demonstrating how to use them for teaching and learning and for personal use;

3. being proactive in fostering twenty-first-century learning skills in the context of the general curriculum and in partnership with the classroom teacher as well as other teaching professionals;

4. providing leadership in the areas of technology integration and inquiry-based, learner-centered education in the school and district;

5. playing an active role in local, regional, and/or national professional organizations; and

6. acting as a role model for and supporter of the ethical use of information in all its forms.

Our final scenario illustrates this shift in roles and responsibilities.

SCENARIO #3: TODAY

It is the current year. Serena Robinson is the school librarian at Main Street School in Collegetown, New York. Due to shrinking enrollments, the elementary and middle schools have merged and the school now serves students in grades K–8. In addition, the community has experienced changes in demographics due to the relocation of a large corporate headquarters to the area and the classes are more diverse and larger to accommodate these changes. Ms. Robinson has worked hard to make sure that students in the school have access to a full range of information resources and technologies. Her library now encompasses an adjoining computer lab and she has spent much of her morning developing a portal of websites and databases for students who will visit the library this week. She is updating her library blog for teachers and parents to showcase information about new library resources, special programs in the library, and exemplary student work. All four of the eighth grade classes are scheduled to come to the library later in the week to learn about some of the new databases that they can use for their research assignments and projects. Serena will visit two of the second grade classrooms with her book cart and laptop to deliver book talks on some new poetry books and show students a brief web-based video on how to create an e-book. This is part of her collaboration with the second grade teachers on an assignment for which students are expected to develop e-books of original poems. During the sixth grade team meeting, Serena demonstrates some ideas for assessing students' projects on the history of New York State, using some of the new Web 2.0 tools. At the end of the day, sixth-grader Sam comes into the library to talk to Ms. Robinson about his research on New York State and how interested he has become in the Haudenosaunees. Sam is curious about the Haudenosaunee tribes in their part of the state and if technology has had an effect on their culture and traditions. Ms. Robinson helps guide Sam's exploration of this topic. Together they find some books on the topic in the library and through interlibrary loan, as well as several websites, including one with video interviews with Haudenosaunee children Sam's age and another that has audio recordings of different Haudenosaunee customs.

Teaching and Learning in the Twenty-First Century

Citizens of the twenty-first century must be able to adapt to and flourish in our fast-paced and ever-changing information- and technology-centered world. While our students face increasing expectations as they follow the path to higher education and/or the workforce, their success is dependent upon having the skills to think flexibly, critically, creatively, and ethically, as well as understand when and how to use these skills, while seeking and using information for learning and working. As a result, school librarians will continue to expand their role as *change agents and educational leaders* into the foreseeable future, while maintaining their basic responsibility: to create "joyful places of learning" (Stripling, 1996: 654) for every student in the school.

Overview of This Book

Teaching for Inquiry: Engaging the Learner Within is intended for both current and future librarians as they prepare for or carry out their instructional role as twenty-first-century school librarians. For the novice or pre-service librarian, it provides a step-by-step guide to instructional design, emphasizing the importance of fostering a motivation for and excitement about learning. In addition, for more experienced information professionals, it provides a twenty-first-century perspective on teaching and learning in which new media and technologies play such an important role. Therefore, this book may be used as a textbook in pre-service library preparation programs or as a reference for current practitioners. Furthermore, while this book is intended for the school librarian, it is also useful to academic, public, and special librarians as well as classroom teachers and parents of homeschoolers.

The authors take the reader through the instructional planning process using an inquiry-based, constructivist, motivational lens. As a result, readers will not only learn to design inquiry-based instruction to meet the information needs of their learners, but will also do so in a way that fosters curiosity, interest, and intrinsically motivated engagement before, during, and after the learning experience.

While the I+M-PACT (**I**nquiry + **M**otivation—**P**urpose, **A**udience, **C**ontent, **T**echnique) Model (Small, 2005) forms the framework for this book, the model has undergone extensive pilot-testing and an evolution that shifts the design focus from information to inquiry and the context to include both inquiry-based teaching and learning. The importance of both inquiry and motivation for library and information skills instruction is explained in detail in Chapter 1, "**I**nquiry + **M**otivation Lead to Deep Understanding."

Chapter 2, "**P**urpose: Beginning at the End," describes the importance of establishing clear goals for student learning and motivation and explains the concepts of backward design and outcome-based evaluation as approaches to instructional planning. The chapter demonstrates the importance of assessing the needs of learners before planning instruction, describes the various levels of cognition, and explains ways to use the AASL *Standards for the 21st-Century Learner* as a guide for designing and organizing instruction, including transforming benchmarks into appropriate learning assessments. Some ideas for fostering librarian-classroom teacher collaboration are provided and the reader is made aware of some potential barriers to successful instructional planning.

Chapter 3, "Students as Learning **A**udience," describes specific characteristics of learners, including their cognitive styles, learning styles, and incoming motivations, in the context of implications for how to design inquiry-based instruction. The reader will learn how to create a motivational profile of a group or class and how motivation relates to the dispositions included in the AASL *Standards for the 21st-Century Learner*. The chapter also looks at how some environmental aspects of teaching and learning can affect students' inquiry success and motivation for learning.

Chapter 4, "Selecting and Organizing **C**ontent," focuses on how to determine the amount, scope, and organization of the information to present in a lesson. Chapter 4 emphasizes the importance of aligning library instruction with the school's curriculum and students' information needs when selecting instructional content. The chapter includes a detailed description of various types of information and skills to teach and scaffold for inquiry as well as some methods for organizing content, once it is selected, and for assessing learning.

Chapter 5, "**T**echnique for Inquiry Teaching and Learning," explores a variety of teaching techniques, methods, and learning-support materials and activities with a special emphasis on the use of new technologies for teaching and learning for inquiry. This chapter demonstrates ways in which a range of technologies may be used to provide differentiated instruction to meet the needs of students with varying abilities. Methods for evaluating the impact of inquiry-skills instructional programs are provided.

Chapter 6, "Bringing It All Together," is a culminating chapter that summarizes the I+M-PACT model as presented. It also allows readers to try out some of the ideas in the book and assessments to demonstrate what they have learned.

Three appendixes provide a survey of perceived competence in information skills, a lesson planning template, and a "Tipping the Scales Worksheet" for goal achievement.

Presentation Conventions

This book uses several standards of presentation, or *conventions*. At the beginning of Chapters 1–5, you will find a brief *situation* that introduces the main theme of the chapter. *Essential Questions* act as advance organizers to the chapter content, followed by the chapter's *Outcomes and Indicators* that readers are expected to achieve after reading the chapter.

Chapters 1–5 each end with an episode of our ongoing case study, starring our fictional librarian Harry Sanchez and classroom teacher Sally Attridge (additional episodes are available on the I+M-PACT website), followed by some questions that stimulate your thinking about the ramifications of Sally and Harry's latest encounter. Following the list of the chapter's references is a special feature called *Digging Deeper* that provides suggested additional resources related to the chapter's content, intended as enrichment for the motivated reader.

In addition, throughout each chapter you will find some or all of the following special features:

- *Stop! Think! Do!*: Brief activity related to the content just addressed
- *Checkpoint*: Recap of recent content presented
- *Words of Wisdom*: Tips for success
- *Taking Action*: Challenges for application of the concepts and processes described in the chapter to an authentic context

Complementary Website

We hope that this book will provide information and ideas that will stimulate creativity and ideas for designing motivating inquiry-based instruction and learning in your library. In order to find a way to demonstrate "in action" some of the ideas and techniques presented in this book and to offer opportunities for going beyond the book's content to learn more about topics you found particularly interesting, we have developed a complementary website, titled *I+M-PACT on the Web*, found at http://teachingforinquiry.net. The I+M-PACT website includes additional examples of strategies described in this book, links to specific lessons and unit plans, online K–12 lessons and teaching ideas from the freely accessible *S.O.S for Information Literacy* database and from the e-book *From the Creative Minds of 21st Century Librarians*, as well as links to relevant articles and websites, and special features to enhance the book's content.

The Author Team

This book is the result of the collaborative and collective synergy of the author team. Each author brought her own unique and special knowledge and experience to the effort and the book's results are greater than the sum of its parts.

The powerful teaming of these four dynamic educators brings together strengths in the areas of curiosity and motivation, inquiry learning, creativity and innovative thinking, and applications of information technology in education. This synergistic collaboration, sharing their research and real-world experiences, results in a unique approach to and perspective on the topic of twenty-first-century teaching and learning and the formal and informal roles and responsibilities of the twenty-first-century school librarian.

References

Small, Ruth V. 2005. *Designing Digital Literacy Programs with IM-PACT: Information Motivation, Purpose, Audience, Content, and Technique.* New York: Neal-Schuman.

Stripling, Barbara K. 1996. "Quality in School Library Media Programs: Focus on Learning." *Library Trends* 44, no. 3: 631–656.

Inquiry + Motivation Lead to Deep Understanding

The eighth graders were finishing their reports to their classmates about the research they had done on aspects of the Civil War. They had listened to a litany of facts for the past five days, and most students had greatly increased the amount of information they knew about the war. It was time to move to the next unit. Then Maria tentatively raised her hand and asked, "But why is it called the 'Civil War'? And why do we care what happened so long ago?"

Introduction

Maria's naïve questions actually get to the heart of teaching and learning in our libraries and classrooms today. Information surrounds us and, through technology, it is increasingly at our fingertips. The accumulation and organization of information has been defined as knowledge; many who write about education have proclaimed that the goal of education is the acquisition of knowledge. Maria and her classmates had gathered information; they had even perhaps organized the information in their heads so that they gained some knowledge about the Civil War. Their information and knowledge, however, did not fulfill the real vision that many educators hold for students' learning—the conversion of knowledge to deep understanding.

Fulfilling that vision for student learning starts with framing the learning in a way that all students are engaged and, at the same time, challenged to think deeply. Both inquiry and motivation are essential components of instruction that pushes students to reach for deep understanding.

Essential Question

This first chapter is grounded in student learning and guided by this essential question:

- How does the combination of inquiry and motivation lead to deep understanding?

Chapter Outcomes and Indicators

By the end of this chapter and through consulting this book's companion website (http://teaching forinquiry.net), you will achieve the following outcomes and indicators:

1. OUTCOME: Develop a commitment to the power of inquiry-based learning and an understanding of an inquiry model.

    a. INDICATOR: Understand the basis of inquiry in learning theory.

    b. INDICATOR: Recall the six phases of the inquiry process.

2. OUTCOME: Understand motivational theory and the importance of infusing motivation into instruction.

    a. INDICATOR: Explain the difference between intrinsic and extrinsic motivation.

    b. INDICATOR: Generate motivational strategies that address each of the four major elements of the ARCS Model of Motivational Design.

    c. INDICATOR: Design ways to foster the development of dispositions.

3. OUTCOME: Design inquiry motivation learning experiences.

    a. INDICATOR: Describe how learning theories have influenced the development of inquiry-based teaching and learning.

    b. INDICATOR: Design constructivist teaching strategies that align with the phases of the inquiry process.

    c. INDICATOR: Assess the learning environment in the library for its inquiry-motivation characteristics.

4. OUTCOME: Understand the I+M-PACT Model.

    a. INDICATOR: Describe the design components of the I+M-PACT Model.

Teaching for Understanding

The transformation of information to knowledge and knowledge to understanding does not happen without the intervention of good teaching. You, as school librarians, are at the forefront of teaching for understanding. The skills and dispositions that you teach are those that enable students to be active and independent learners who make sense of the information they read, see, and hear in order to draw their own conclusions and apply them to new situations. Through the processes of application and constructive thinking, learners convert information and knowledge to understanding.

Teaching for understanding is not easy, nor is it a one-size-fits-all approach to instructional design. Two main aspects will help you develop an instructional program in the library that engages learners and fosters understanding: framing around inquiry-based teaching and learning and infusing motivational strategies.

Teaching for understanding in the library requires a balance between the classroom teacher's priorities and the students' needs and interests. You are in a prime position to navigate that balance by collaborating with the teachers to establish high expectations for content learning and collaborating with the students to integrate their needs and interests into the inquiry investigations. By starting with high expectations for learning and attention to student and teacher needs, you can develop instruction that blends inquiry with motivation, the formula for teaching for understanding.

> *Teaching for Understanding =*
> *Inquiry + Motivation*

Context of Curriculum

Inquiry and motivation are teaching and learning processes that have full value when they are wedded to content, whether the student is pursuing individual topics of interest or completing class assignments. When students are simply browsing the Internet idly, flitting from subject to subject and cruising from site to site, picking up extraneous and unconnected facts (usually about topics of current popular interest), they are not really learning.

You, as a librarian, know from experience that students do not learn skills and behaviors unless they have a reason to learn and understand. The curriculum of the school (and teaching it in a way that demonstrates its relevance to students) offers that important context. When instruction in the library is targeted to the skills most appropriate for learning the classroom content, then students develop greater understandings, both in content and in skills. Library literature stresses the essential nature of collaboration with teachers, not only to foster access to the library, but also to ensure that the teaching of skills is embedded with the content to be learned and real learning ensues.

Framing around Inquiry-Based Teaching and Learning

The Concept of Inquiry

Inquiry forms the root of various teaching and learning paradigms held by teachers and librarians, including discovery learning, problem-based learning, project-based learning, and active learning in addition to inquiry learning. These varied applications have led to confusion in the scope and practice of inquiry and have resulted in a lack of careful implementation. We must, therefore, define clearly what we mean by inquiry-based learning as well as the learning environment and teaching strategies that will enable students to pursue inquiry.

Inquiry is a process for learning that involves connecting to personal interests and a desire to know, gaining background knowledge, asking questions that probe beyond simple fact gathering, investigating answers to gather evidence from multiple perspectives and sources, constructing new understandings and drawing conclusions with support from evidence, expressing the new ideas through a variety of formats, and reflecting metacognitively on both the process and product of learning. Inquiry is recursive and cyclical, with learners going back and forth between the phases to resolve new questions and complexities as they arise. True inquiry should result in new understandings for learners, but not final answers, because during the process, learners should naturally restimulate their curiosity and discover new questions and intriguing areas to pursue in future investigations. Perhaps there is no better result from an inquiry investigation than the comment, "Ah, I understand, but now I wonder…"

The Reason for Inquiry

The ability to solve problems and use information literacy skills to pursue inquiry-based learning has increasingly been identified as critical to the twenty-first century, not just by educators, but also by business leaders and professionals in every content area. The Partnership for 21st Century Skills, with an advisory board of prominent business, professional, and technology organizations, has published a framework that identifies the skills of learning and innovation and the information, media, and technology skills that are essential to teaching and learning (Partnership for 21st Century Skills, 2003). A librarian in British Columbia, William Badke, sums up the importance of inquiry (Badke, 2009: 55):

The ability to work with information, whether in written, audio, or video form—to define a problem, understand the nature of the information available, use the best tools well to find the information needed, and then enlist the information effectively and ethically to address the issue at hand—may well be the most important skill of the 21st century.

Learning Theories behind Inquiry

Inquiry didn't just pop up as an important concept in learning; it evolved from a line of educational theory and research. Three main theories may be of interest because of their impact on inquiry-based teaching and learning: John Dewey's (1938) series of connected experiences; Lev Vygotsky's (1978) Zone of Proximal Development; and Jerome Bruner's (1986) emphasis on interpretation in learning.

John Dewey believed that learners derive meaning by engaging in a series of connected experiences that cause them to hypothesize, reflect, and explore. The teacher's role is to select experiences that "have the promise and potentiality of presenting new problems which by stimulating new ways of observations and judgment will expand the area of further experience" (Dewey, 1938: 75). In other words, Dewey recognized that we all learn through experience, that one experience leads to another, and that, although the teacher prepares the environment, the learner determines his own learning. Dewey's philosophy is the foundation of what we now call constructivism, an educational approach aligned with inquiry-based learning, in which the learner actively investigates and constructs his own meaning.

Lev Vygotsky's learning theory called the Zone of Proximal Development (ZPD) has implications for inquiry-based learning, but also for inquiry-based teaching by the school librarian. The ZPD represents the gap between the level that learners can reach on their own and the level they can achieve with provocation and scaffolding from a knowledgeable "other" (Vygotsky, 1978). Learners do not reach the upper region of their "Zone" without both provocation and support. The ZPD is a Zone of Intervention for the librarian (Kuhlthau, 2004). Librarians must challenge students to reach higher levels of thinking and at the same time provide the emotional and cognitive supports that enable students to reach those levels.

Psychologist Jerome Bruner also offers theories on the nature of learning that confirm the importance of inquiry. Bruner says that knowledge is not embedded within the content but is constructed by the learner through social interaction (Bruner, 1986). Bruner believes that students should be engaged in active inquiry, examining diverse perspectives and drawing their own interpretations.

School libraries, then, have a unique combination of influences that enable you, as the school librarian, to lead the focus on inquiry-based teaching and learning. Instead of being limited to the traditional resource provider role, you can redefine your role to that of provocateur and supporter of inquiry-based learning. Education theorists Dewey, Vygotsky, and Bruner describe a vision for learning in today's school libraries—experience-based, thoughtful, interactive, and challenging. Framing instruction around an inquiry process and teaching the skills of inquiry are important contributions of librarians to student engagement and learning.

An Inquiry Model

The process-model approach to learning and inquiry has evolved quite naturally in the school library field since the 1980s when librarians and library educators began to focus on a research process and information literacy skills. Carol Kuhlthau published a seven-step research process, the only such process based on longitudinal research with students, in her 1985 book titled *Teaching the Library Research Process.* Her process was later revised to become the Information Search Process (ISP) model. Over the past 25 years, the school library field has been replete with variations of research process models, but the increasing importance of constructivism, authentic learning, and inquiry have led some process developers to shift from linear research processes to recursive and cyclical inquiry processes (e.g., the Pathways to Knowledge model developed by Marjorie Pappas and Ann Tepe, 2002; the Stripling Inquiry Model, Stripling, 2003).

Based largely on constructivist learning theory, one of the authors (Stripling) has developed an inquiry model with the following phases: Connect, Wonder, Investigate, Construct, Express, and Reflect (Stripling, 2003). Specific thinking strategies and actions characterize each phase, although the whole process is recursive and overlapping (see Figure 1.1). The Stripling model resembles the cognitive aspects of Kuhlthau's information-seeking ISP model, but it places greater emphasis on certain stages of the process—questioning rather than selecting a topic as the impetus for the investigation; the construction of interpretations and conclusions after information is collected; and final reflection of the learner.

Process models of research and inquiry are firmly embedded in the school library field. You can plan instructional units with classroom teachers using a process model of inquiry as a frame for the design, resources, and instruction in information skills.

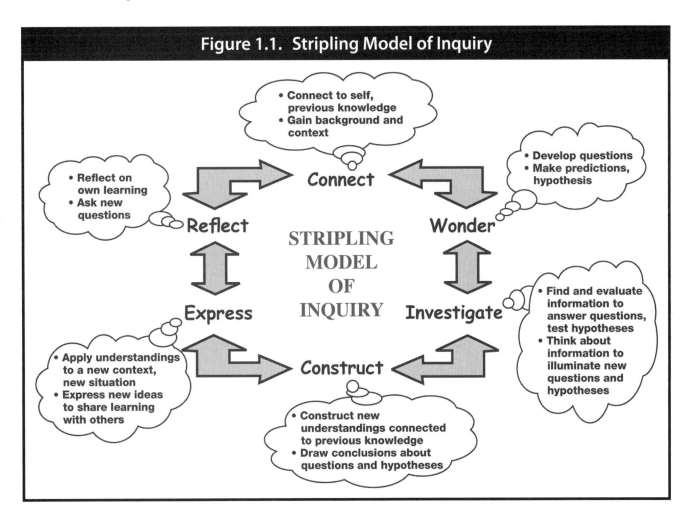

Figure 1.1. Stripling Model of Inquiry

Teaching Inquiry-Based Skills

Students need to develop a wide array of skills to pursue inquiry effectively—not only "traditional" research skills, but also literacy, critical thinking, technology, and digital literacy and inquiry skills. These skills have been defined by standards documents from a number of organizations. National standards from the American Association of School Librarians, *Standards for the 21st-Century Learner* (AASL, 2007) emphasize the importance of inquiry skills for effective learning. AASL's standards and indicators highlight the skills that enable students to find and think critically about information in all formats and to create and share their new understandings. The Common Core State Standards Initiative (2010) for literacy includes strands on research, informational reading, and informational writing that embed inquiry skills from kindergarten through twelfth grade.

> **CHECKPOINT**
>
> Inquiry-based teaching and learning are largely based on the work of theorists John Dewey, Lev Vygotsky, and Jerome Bruner. In a school library context, inquiry and constructivist theories formed the foundation for Stripling's (2003) Model of Inquiry and AASL's (2007) *Standards for the 21st-Century Learner.*

Standards from the International Society for Technology in Education (ISTE, 2007) include creativity, communication, research, information fluency, critical thinking, and digital citizenship as well as technology skills. State and local education agencies have developed information curricula to provide coherent guidance for the development of inquiry and information skills in all students. One such local effort in New York City has resulted in a K–12 Information Fluency Continuum with grade-level benchmarks and formative assessments (New York City School Library System, 2010). An excerpt from that Continuum is included in Chapter 4 in the discussion about the content of library instruction.

Framing around Motivational Strategies

The Concept of Motivation

Librarians who wish to teach for understanding will find that the combination of differentiating instruction based on student interests and needs and framing instruction around inquiry leads to infusing motivation. Motivation has been studied and used extensively in the workplace by managers who want to make sure their workers produce the most, the best, or the fastest. Motivation is highly valued by athletic coaches and politicians whose job is to win. Rarely does an unmotivated team or political candidate beat the opponents.

Motivation is a key component in learning; not only does it help promote learning, it is *essential* for deep understanding and long-term learning. By creating engaging and appropriately challenging learning situations, we provide the type of provocative learning environment envisioned by Vygotsky (1978).

The concept of motivation, as described in this book, is broadly conceived to include an understanding of how knowledge can help us be better, faster, and more satisfied learners. Dewey's (1938) emphasis on learning through experience helps to highlight the importance of making learning relevant. Unless you know the reasons for learning, you may not be motivated to transform that knowledge to deep understanding or to use it in new situations.

While it is true that unmotivated students can (and often do) learn and achieve, those same unmotivated students rarely sustain their learning and achievement over time, mainly because that motivation does not flow from within but, rather, is imposed from outside. So, how do you know whether your students are motivated?

Often you'll look for physical cues, such as wide-eyed looks, raised hands, and enthusiastic responses to your questions. But motivation is much more than this; it is an outward demonstration of *effort*. Students may be described as motivated learners when they, as Bruner (1986) described, are actively engaged in the learning process, independently doing more work than is expected, producing higher quality or more work than they previously produced or than was required, or requesting additional or enriched learning opportunities. In constructivist learning environments, this type of student autonomy and initiative is fostered; inventing original solutions and trying out new ideas are rewarded.

Extrinsic and Intrinsic Motivation

Two general types of motivators result in learning effort: extrinsic and intrinsic. The *extrinsic motivator* is induced by external forces such as parents, teachers, or even other students. Some examples of external motivators are praise, rewards, and incentives. Most schoolwork (e.g., assignments, projects) can be considered extrinsically motivated because it originates from the teacher. Whether a teacher awards a prize for completing a learning task, assigns a grade to a learning product, or praises a student's learning effort, all are external to the learner. Incentive programs that offer tangible rewards (e.g., bicycles, pizza parties) for exhibiting motivated behavior (e.g., reading a specified number of books, maintaining good behavior) are also examples of external motivators.

A classroom filled with motivated students is every teacher's dream, but, more likely, the teacher faces a range of motivation levels in any group. Sometimes teachers use extrinsic motivators such as praise and rewards related to the learning task in order to lead students eventually to more *intrinsically motivated behavior* that comes from within and is activated by the learner. For example, praising a student for mastering reading skills may lead to the student's reading for pleasure without any tangible external motivators. Providing recognition for student effort and achievement by displaying children's projects in the library can stimulate continued motivation for exemplary performance.

Extrinsic rewards are short-lived and should be used judiciously, and only until students move to a more intrinsic orientation. In some cases, the use of extrinsic rewards can have a detrimental effect. For example, extensive research by Ed Deci and Rich Ryan (1985) at the University of Rochester revealed that offering rewards for tasks students already find intrinsically motivating (e.g., rewards based on quantity of reading offered to students who already love to read) can actually have a negative effect on intrinsic motivation. The ultimate goal is for students to be motivated by pride in their learning accomplishments and achievements rather than by external rewards.

Motivation Theories Relevant to Inquiry-Based Teaching and Learning

Motivational factors in the educational environment heavily influence the effectiveness of learning. Edward Deci, known for his work on motivation, offers three ideas about intrinsic motivation that will help librarians blend motivation with inquiry to provoke effective learning. First, Deci says that students need to be supported as *autonomous* learners. Instead of pressuring or controlling students, Deci asserts that teachers need to encourage students by offering choices and opportunities to take risks, initiate actions, experiment, and accept responsibility for their own behavior. Support for students' autonomy is especially effective in inquiry-based learning situations: "Intrinsic motivation is associated with richer experience, better conceptual understanding, greater creativity, and improved problem solving, relative to external controls" (Deci and Flaste, 1995: 51).

Deci also states that *competence* is extremely important for intrinsic motivation. When we teach and scaffold the skills of inquiry as a part of learning experiences, students are more likely to be successful and feel competent. Students who feel competent are motivated to engage in inquiry: "When you think about it, the curiosity of children—their intrinsic motivation to learn—might, to a large extent, be attributed to their need to feel effective or competent in dealing with their world" (Deci and Flaste, 1995: 65). The motivation that comes from a feeling of competence also requires that the learning experience must present enough challenge to spark the desire to learn. Students are motivated when they encounter and overcome learning situations that require them to stretch their capacities and develop new understandings.

Deci and Flaste (1995) identify a third factor in intrinsic motivation—*relatedness*. Students will be more motivated to pursue inquiry when they feel connected to each other and part of a social context. Later in this chapter, you will find a Self-Assessment Rubric to determine how conducive your library is to inquiry learning. A section of that rubric, the Social/Emotional Environment, includes characteristics of the intrinsic motivation factor of relatedness (e.g., opportunities for social interaction and shared learning).

Victor Vroom (1994) and others have conducted research based on a theory that suggests that value and an expectation for success are prerequisites for putting forth an intrinsically motivated effort. This theory is called *expectancy-value theory* (E-V theory).

Applied to a learning context, expectancy-value theory may be stated that learners must first value the learning task; that is, the task must have some personal meaning, importance, or usefulness to the individual. Learners must also believe that they have a reasonable chance of succeeding at the learning task, and this belief is reinforced through feelings of competence and confidence. In addition, *you*, the instructor, must also believe it and you hold much power in making it happen. Noted motivation researcher Deborah Stipek states, "To a very large degree, students expect to learn if their teachers expect them to learn" (Stipek and Daniels, 1988: 352). For many students, learning success (or failure) can become a type of self-fulfilling prophecy.

In E-V theory, *both* of these prerequisites must be present for learners to be *intrinsically* motivated. Students who value what they are learning but don't think they are capable of learning it are not likely to be highly motivated to put forth effort. Similarly, students who believe they can do the task but don't find it particularly relevant to their needs will probably not extend much effort toward the task. But students who believe that the learning is valuable and that they can be successful are likely to be motivated students. This theory forms the basis of a simple yet powerful model of motivational design, the ARCS Model of Motivational Design.

The ARCS Model of Motivational Design

The ARCS Model of Motivational Design (aka the ARCS Model), developed by John Keller (1987), professor emeritus of instructional systems at Florida State University, is a prescriptive model that identifies four major elements of motivating instruction. As you continue reading about each of the four elements, you might want to think about some related teaching strategies you might use to create challenging and engaging inquiry-based instruction for your students.

- The first ARCS element is Attention, stimulating students' curiosity, engaging their attention, and maintaining their interest throughout the learning experience and continuing after the instruction has ended.

- The second ARCS element is Relevance and, we believe, probably the most important of the ARCS components. Providing relevance requires methods that help learners understand the importance and usefulness of the learning in their lives now and into the future.

- The third ARCS element is Confidence. Confidence is built when the student experiences learning success and feelings of competence that are reinforced through feedback at various points throughout the learning process.

- The final ARCS element is Satisfaction. Creating a potentially satisfying learning environment builds on the other three elements; it is that feeling of accomplishment when a learning challenge has been successfully achieved. It is through learning satisfaction that students develop a continuing motivation and love of learning.

In their research study, Small and Gluck (1994) found a significant relationship between the attention and relevance elements of the ARCS Model and the value component of expectancy-value theory. This means that by exposing students to curiosity-stimulating, interesting, and meaningful learning situations, students are more likely to value the learning task.

Small and Gluck found a similarly strong relationship between the confidence and satisfaction elements of ARCS and the expectancy for success component of E-V theory. This indicates that learning situations in which students can develop a confidence in their ability to achieve a learning task and feel a sense of satisfaction in the effort they put forth and level of achievement they reached will contribute to a strong expectancy for success in future learning challenges.

No child comes to school thinking, "I think I'll fail today." Every child wants to enjoy the positive feelings resulting from learning success, but not every child has developed the intrinsic motivation (through successful learning) to accomplish that. As school librarians, it is not your responsibility to motivate students, but rather to "create the conditions within which (students) will motivate themselves" (Deci and Flaste, 1995: 10). Throughout this book, you will find examples of ways in which you can apply motivational strategies from each of the ARCS Model's elements to design learning environments that foster students' development of positive dispositions in the context of inquiry-based learning.

> **CHECKPOINT**
>
> A number of motivation theories and concepts are directly relevant to inquiry-based teaching and learning, such as expectancy-value theory, intrinsic motivation, and self-determination theory. The ARCS Model of Motivational Design is particularly applicable to inquiry-based teaching and learning in a library context. This model prescribes motivational teaching strategies that gain and maintain Attention, promote Relevance, build Confidence, and guarantee Satisfaction for learners.

Fostering the Development of Dispositions

Students are highly motivated and engaged by learning that is inquiry based, challenging, and meaningful. The attitudes, values, and expectations students have before, during, and after they complete a learning task are expressions of students' motivation toward learning. These emotions, thoughts, beliefs, and attitudes are called dispositions; students' dispositions toward learning often result in almost predictable patterns of response, even when students are not making a conscious decision to dig a little deeper or work a little harder. For example, students who are disposed to persevere will pursue their investigations beyond setbacks or challenges—they will keep looking for sources to answer their questions when the first sources they find are inadequate.

The American Association of School Librarians (AASL) identified dispositions as one of four important strands influencing all learning, the other three being skills, responsibilities, and self-assessment strategies (AASL, 2007). A variety of educational writers have identified the important influence of dispositions in successful learning. Art Costa and Bena Kallick called them "habits of mind," which they defined as "having a disposition towards solving a problem to which the solution is not readily apparent" (Costa and Kallick, 2001: 2).

David Conley published a research study in 2005 that defines the habits of mind needed by first-year students to succeed in university work, including critical thinking, analytic thinking, problem solving, inquisitive nature, ability to deal with frustrating and ill-formed problems, drawing inferences and conclusions, and using technology to assist in learning (Conley, 2005: 173). Deborah Meier places dispositions in the context of the twenty-first century: "Educating kids for the 21st century means teaching them the habits of mind that will help them benefit from—and be benefits to—the world" (Meier, 2003: 16).

Because dispositions are expressed through actions, teachers (and the students themselves) can assess how well students have developed dispositions that lead to effective inquiry and motivated learning. Students do not develop dispositions like curiosity and empathy automatically. Young people may have a cognitive grasp of the skills of inquiry and a knowledge of motivational factors, but only when they develop the dispositions to use their skills and look within themselves for motivation do they begin to display intrinsic motivation to pursue independent inquiry.

Dispositions, like motivation, are not explicitly taught. The challenge for librarians and classroom teachers is to design learning experiences and construct learning environments that empower young people to practice and adopt the dispositions that support inquiring and motivated minds. "Over time, through a series of experiences that reinforce the targeted attitudes and behaviors, students will adopt the dispositions as their own personal habits of mind" (Stripling, 2008: 48).

> **TAKING ACTION**
>
> Can you think of some inquiry-based, motivating teaching strategies that you might use to foster one or more of the dispositions?

Instructional Design for Inquiry + Motivation: The I+M-PACT Model

The instructional program in libraries is founded on a synergy of inquiry and motivation, and the library environment is conducive to the development of both. Inquiry-based learning provides students with opportunities for independent, active learning and leads them to in-depth understanding. Such learning is highly motivating to students because they can adapt the process and content focus to their differentiated needs and interests, while they learn to employ inquiry skills in the pursuit of new understandings.

Effective instructional designs, whether for single lessons or entire units, start with the expected learning outcomes of the students—what they are supposed to understand and be able to do at the end of the instruction. Skill development is fostered through both instruction and time for practice. With enough practice, students convert their positive attitudes and their competence in skills to habits of mind that open the door to lifelong learning.

As we saw in our three scenarios in the preface, changes in the information and technology world have led to a rethinking of the library's role in providing access to resources and tools for learning. Although physical access to resources has been greatly enhanced by the digital environment, students' intellectual access has become more complex, with added skills required for thoughtful access and use of digital text, images, and tools. Interactive social tools have opened the door to enhanced collaboration among students and teachers, but have at the same time presented new challenges in the arena of social responsibility and ethical use of information.

Overview of I+M-PACT Model

This book is organized around the I+M-PACT model of instructional design. The I+M-PACT model has inquiry and motivation at its core, requiring that both the teaching and learning strategies of inquiry and the principles of motivation frame the instructional program in the library, resulting in experiences that excite students' intellectual curiosity, stimulate their inquiry behavior, foster the development of dispositions, and motivate a lifelong quest for understanding and creating new knowledge.

The I+M-PACT model is based on the PACT Model for Designing Effective Information Presentations (Small and Arnone, 2002), applied to a constructivist learning environment in the library. The model, however, can be applied to any discipline, level, or context; therefore, you are encouraged to share the model with your teaching colleagues.

One aspect of the model is different from any other instructional design model—inquiry and motivation are incorporated throughout the instructional design process. That process includes four essential design components: **P**urpose (Why?), **A**udience (Who?), **C**ontent (What?), and **T**echnique (How?).

These four components do not represent a step-by-step process but rather a highly dynamic and iterative one in which you must clearly understand your purpose and your learning audience *before* you begin to determine what content you will present and the technique you will use to deliver the content. Sometimes you will need to reconsider your purpose once you have identified your audience and determined your content and technique. Similarly, the content you include and the technique(s) you choose will be highly influenced by your purpose and what you know about your audience. As your audience's needs change, you must rethink the other components—thus the iterative nature of the model. The interdependence of the four PACT design components is illustrated in Figure 1.2.

To define the purpose of your instructional presentation, you must determine why instruction is needed and exactly what outcomes you expect your students to gain—what they should understand and be able to do at the end of the learning experience. You will also discover in Chapter 2 that inquiry skills learning extends beyond simple content to include motivational goals.

As you identify the purpose of your instruction, you will also need to consider your learning audience. Who are the students for this learning experience? What are their strengths and needs? This is sometimes referred to as

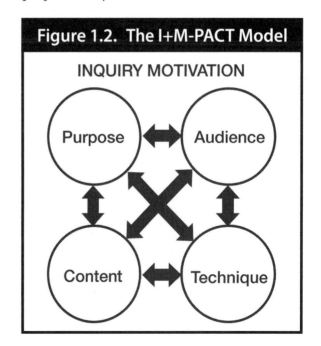

Figure 1.2. The I+M-PACT Model

INQUIRY MOTIVATION

Purpose ⟷ Audience

Content ⟷ Technique

"audience analysis." Chapter 3 guides you through the audience analysis process so that you can plan a lesson or unit that empowers student learning.

Knowledge of the purpose and audience for your instruction provides the basis for determining what and how much content to select and how to organize that content. Chapter 4 gives some ideas for selecting and organizing the amount, type, and scope of content you include in your lesson or unit as well as how to assess the learning of that content. At the same time, you'll need to decide how you might effectively deliver that content through teaching techniques and the use of technology, the subject of Chapter 5. Chapter 6 contains a lesson-planning guide that you can complete as you design instruction using the I+M-PACT model.

Designing Inquiry + Motivation Learning Experiences

The combination of inquiry and motivation produces active thinking and learning, a concept first proposed by John Dewey (Dewey, 1938) and adopted and adapted by many educational theorists over the years. The current educational philosophy that retains some of the most effective behaviorist and experiential principles at its foundation but emphasizes the active learning component is called constructivism.

Constructivist Learning

Inquiry-based learning is an effective application of constructivism. Your students will actively *construct* (rather than passively *acquire*) knowledge and understanding by integrating new information with their prior knowledge and experience. The skills and processes of inquiry will enable your students to learn by doing through direct, hands-on engagement in the learning process in real or simulated situations. Your students must be able to reflect on their prior experiences and develop questions to investigate new ideas; plan and conduct learning and research activities; seek, evaluate, make meaning from, and organize information; think critically and creatively; and monitor their own understanding (see Table 1.1, p. 15). These skills and processes of inquiry foster autonomy and self-directed learning. As a result, students are motivated to learn.

Two other aspects of inquiry-based, constructivist learning will motivate and empower your students—engagement in authentic tasks and assessments and learning through social interaction. Inquiry learning is typically assessed through performance-based projects and activities rather than through traditional paper-and-pencil testing. The most meaningful learning emerges from authentic performance tasks. Imagine how differently your students will engage if they can present a "live" news report of the Lewis and Clark expedition to their classmates instead of a written report that they submit to their classroom teacher.` A more in-depth look at assessment tasks and products is offered in Chapters 2 and 4.

Learning is also enhanced through social interactivity. When you offer students opportunities to collaborate, during both the process of inquiry and the presentation of the final product, you motivate them to engage. Motivation, in fact, may be the critical variable in understanding why two learners in the same learning situation may exhibit different learning behaviors and produce different learning outcomes (Venkatesh, Small, and Marsden, 2003). Steinberg (1996: 15) writes that boredom and "disengagement" of the learner, which he defines as "the degree to which students are psychologically 'connected' to what is going on in their classes," is pervasive in today's schools. He goes on to state that only the constructivist learning environment addresses this issue because it is a learner-centered, dynamic, and active learning environment in which students are energized and collaborative.

Constructivist Teaching

Constructivist teaching is a process for supporting learner-constructed (rather than teacher-communicated) knowledge and understanding (Duffy and Cunningham, 1996; Jaeger and Lauritzen, 1992). As a school librarian, you know that your role is that of facilitator or coach, guiding students and stimulating and provoking their critical thinking, analysis, and synthesis throughout the learning process, not that of a conveyor of information and knowledge. You maintain a balance in your teaching between provocation and support, both pushing students to meet high expectations and facilitating their learning through scaffolding and guidance. As a constructivist teacher librarian, you:

- seek to understand students' mental models and any assumptions used to support them;
- foster collaboration (and model it), motivating students through active participation;
- provide reassurance and encouragement to students, when needed;
- ask hard questions to push students to deeper understanding; and
- act as a "guide on the side" by interacting with students and helping them to find information, rather than as a "sage on the stage" by providing information and doing the thinking and work for the students.

Carol Kuhlthau (1993) found that the constructivist perspective's emphases on reflection, reconstruction, and interpretation provide a particularly useful framework for her notable research into the information-search process. Likewise, inquiry skills instruction, with its emphases on authentic learning experiences, integration with the curriculum, and collaboration between classroom teachers and librarians, seems particularly well suited to constructivist learning experiences.

In the often-cited book about the science of learning, *How People Learn*, the editors build upon the research about learning to offer three main areas to be considered in teaching: prior knowledge; in-depth learning; and reflection and metacognition (Bransford, Brown, and Cocking, 2000). When you are designing inquiry-based, constructivist instruction, you will want to pay attention to these three areas:

- **Prior Knowledge:** Start with what the students already know and help them construct new understandings from that platform, either replacing misconceptions or deepening the conceptions they already had.
  - *Start the inquiry with a Connect experience by eliciting what students already know about the topic through group sharing, concept maps, or filling out the "Know" portion of a Know-Wonder-Learn (K-W-L) chart.*
  - *Build background knowledge by asking students to read or view general encyclopedia articles, overview periodical articles, video excerpts, or broad overviews in textbooks or trade books.*
  - *Give students a diagnostic assessment at the beginning of an inquiry unit to bring to the surface any misconceptions that they hold about the topic. If those misconceptions are not made explicit, students will probably not change them, even if they find conflicting information.*

- **In-Depth Learning:** Foster deep learning about major concepts in the curriculum, building on a base of content knowledge and providing multiple opportunities for students to grapple with the ideas to build in-depth understanding.
  - *Use concepts and essential questions as the base for designing inquiry-based instructional units.*
  - *Start the instructional design process by defining the expected learning outcomes (what do you want students to understand and be able to do at the end of the inquiry experience?) and planning backwards from there.*
  - *Include consideration of multiple perspectives and opposing points of view whenever appropriate so that students have to form their own opinions and reach their own conclusions.*
  - *Structure the lessons and activities so that students have to construct their own understanding, apply it to new situations, and express their understanding in creative products that cannot be copied.*

- **Reflection and Metacognition:** Provide opportunities and time for students to reflect, to think metacognitively about their own learning. Research shows that integrating metacognitive instruction with discipline-based teaching, grounded in an inquiry cycle, helps students become independent learners and improves their achievement and level of understanding (Bransford, Brown, and Cocking, 2000).
  - *Teach students reflective techniques to be used throughout their inquiry experience, such as two-column note taking, use of process rubrics, and peer sharing and feedback.*
  - *Provide opportunities and tools for students to assess their own work.*
  - *Give students reflective questions to be used throughout the inquiry cycle. Reflective questions developed by the New York City School Library System (2010) may be seen in Table 1.1.*

Designing Motivating Inquiry-Based Learning Environments

Inquiry-based learning experiences that motivate students to develop new understandings depend on the learning environment for their effectiveness. *How People Learn* uses the research about learning to describe four general characteristics of an effective learning environment that supports deep and reflective learning (Bransford, Brown, and Cocking, 2000). The learning environment should be:

1. learner-centered (focused on the skills, knowledge, attitudes, and beliefs that students bring with them to the classroom);

2. knowledge-centered (well-organized discipline-based knowledge and an emphasis on sense-making);

3. assessment-centered (formative assessments with feedback, self-assessment, and authentic summative assessments); and

4. community-centered (sense of community created in the classroom as well as connections to the broader community) (Bransford, Brown, and Cocking, 2000).

The last characteristic of an effective learning environment—community-centered—captures an important and fundamental aspect of learning that may be overlooked in the focus on individual learners: the understanding that learning is social. Lev Vygotsky recognized the interdependence between the individual and his social milieu. To Vygotsky, individuals learn and

Table 1.1. Reflective Questions for Inquiry Cycle

INQUIRY PHASE: CONNECT

At the beginning of the Connect Phase, a student may ask: ➤ What interests me about this idea or topic? ➤ What do I already know or think I know about this topic? ➤ What background information would help me get an overview of my topic?	*Before moving to the Wonder Phase, a student may ask:* ➤ Do I know enough about the idea or topic to ask good questions? ➤ Am I interested enough in the idea or topic to investigate it?

INQUIRY PHASE: WONDER

At the beginning of the Wonder Phase, a student may ask: ➤ What intriguing questions do I have about the topic or idea? ➤ Why am I doing this research? ➤ What do I expect to find?	*Before moving to the Investigate Phase, a student may ask:* ➤ Can my question(s) be answered through investigation? ➤ Will my question(s) lead me to answers that will fulfill my assignment or purpose for research?

INQUIRY PHASE: INVESTIGATE

At the beginning of the Investigate Phase, a student may ask: ➤ What are all of the sources that might be used? ➤ Which sources will be most useful and valuable? ➤ How do I locate these sources? ➤ How do I find the information within each source? ➤ How do I evaluate the information that I find?	*Before moving to the Construct Phase, a student may ask:* ➤ Have I located sources with diverse perspectives? ➤ Have I found enough accurate information to answer all my questions? ➤ Have I discovered information gaps and filled them with more research? ➤ Have I begun to identify relationships and patterns and thoughtfully reacted to the information I found?

INQUIRY PHASE: CONSTRUCT

At the beginning of the Construct Phase, a student may ask: ➤ Have any main ideas emerged from the research? ➤ Did I find enough evidence to form an opinion or support my thesis? ➤ What organizational patterns or tools will help me make sense of my information?	*Before moving to the Express Phase, a student may ask:* ➤ Have I drawn conclusions that are supported by the evidence? ➤ Have I organized my conclusions and evidence to present them effectively?

INQUIRY PHASE: EXPRESS

At the beginning of the Express Phase, a student may ask: ➤ What type of product or presentation will allow me to present my conclusions and evidence effectively to the intended audience? ➤ What technology will help me create a product or presentation? ➤ How will I get help to revise and edit my product?	*Before moving to the Reflect Phase, a student may ask:* ➤ Have I organized the product/presentation to make my major points and present convincing evidence? ➤ Does my product/presentation fulfill all the requirements of the assignment?

INQUIRY PHASE: REFLECT

At the beginning of the Reflect Phase, a student may ask: ➤ Is my product/presentation as effective as I can make it? ➤ How well did my inquiry process go? ➤ How can I get feedback on my final product to use in my next inquiry project?	*Before moving to another assignment or personal inquiry, a student may ask:* ➤ What new understandings did I develop about the topic or idea? ➤ What did I learn about inquiry? ➤ What new questions do I now want to answer about the topic or idea?

appropriate ideas internally only when they interact with others in their environment (Vygotsky, 1978). Furthermore, in his more than 20 years of research at Harvard on achievement motivation, David McClelland (e.g., 1987) found that one of the strongest human motivation needs is the need for affiliation; i.e., the need to be involved in and supported by social groups and warm interpersonal interactions. A community-centered learning environment, therefore, also addresses the affiliation needs of learners.

Research shows that participants' thoughts, learning, and knowledge are changed as a result of the social context and the experience of multiple perspectives and social construction of ideas (Duffy and Cunningham, 1996; Palincsar, 1998). When learners explain their thinking to another, it leads to deep thinking (Scardamalia and Bereiter, 1989).

In an ideal world, the essential elements of an effective learning environment are in place in every classroom and school library. As a school librarian, you have the opportunity to design the library environment to focus on your students' needs and interests, engender deep exploration of curriculum content, provide interactive and social learning experiences, and promote the use of technology and high-quality resources. Because of the flexibility of the library environment, you can create a space that fosters the intellectual, social, and emotional growth of your students. Your library can become a community of interactive learning where ideas are both exchanged and challenged and multiple perspectives are respected.

For this to happen, the library must be a safe, inviting, and engaging atmosphere for students and teachers. To create a climate conducive to learning, you can focus on three areas of the environment: physical, intellectual, and social/emotional. You may use the self-assessment rubric in Table 1.2 to assess how well the climate in your library supports inquiry-based learning and student motivation now and how you'd like to change the environment for the future.

> **WORDS OF WISDOM**
>
> One of the best ways to get your teachers involved with your library program is to set up a Library Advisory Committee (LAC). The Climate Self-Assessment Rubric is an effective tool to engage LAC members in thinking about the library space and program as integral and essential to the learning culture of the school. Ask each member of the LAC to complete the assessment, then plan as a committee how you will work together to strengthen the library in the areas that are most important for your school.

Table 1.2. Climate Conducive to Learning: Self-Assessment Rubric

Characteristic	Not Really	Somewhat	Generally True
Physical Environment			
The entrance to the library is inviting and draws students all the way in.			
The facility is well organized and easy for students to find the areas that interest them.			
Displays feature student work and help give students a sense of ownership in the library.			
The physical environment is interesting and interactive, with special displays of books, books turned face out on the shelves, computers and other technologies, and exhibits that feature provoking ideas and themes.			

(Continued)

Table 1.2. Climate Conducive to Learning: Self-Assessment Rubric *(Continued)*			
Characteristic	**Not Really**	**Somewhat**	**Generally True**
Intellectual Environment			
Displays, resources, and programs are designed to answer diverse student interests and needs.			
Students have many opportunities for choice, from participating in the selection of resources for the library to choosing resources they want to use and deciding their own paths of discovery.			
Students have voice in the library through a variety of opportunities: presentation of their work to their peers, debates and discussion groups, sharing of their book reviews and recommendations, book clubs, and group research projects.			
Students are intellectually engaged in inquiry projects and supported by the librarian through whole-class instruction, individual and small-group guidance, and structured peer-to-peer feedback.			
The library is a place of discovery where students are actively confronted with new ideas, conflicting opinions, and challenging but interesting texts.			
Social/Emotional Environment			
Students have many opportunities for social interaction: shared learning, discussions and conversations to exchange ideas, group projects and presentations, and peer feedback.			
The library program integrates activities and resources that motivate students to read and learn.			
Library instructional units are designed to motivate students by engaging their attention, connecting to their lives, offering them opportunities to develop confidence in their own competence, and helping them achieve satisfaction with their own success.			
Rules and procedures in the library facilitate an orderly climate that empowers students to act responsibly and learn on their own.			
Students feel safe in the library to investigate topics of personal concern.			
Students are supported by signage, posted research tips, pathfinders and other scaffolding strategies, and just-in-time help from the librarian to enable them to be successful in their investigations and develop self-confidence in their own ability to be an independent learner.			
Collaboration in the library among students and teachers is encouraged by the arrangement of work spaces, the structure of activities, and the collaborative tone set by the librarian.			
Parents are actively encouraged to visit and participate in the library at designated times.			

Case Study #1: When Harry Met Sally

Harry Sanchez was eager to begin his first year as a school librarian at Davenport Middle School, a school of about 700 students in grades 5–8 in Scottsville, a small city in upstate New York. Just three months earlier, he had received his master's degree in library and information science and, soon thereafter, was selected to serve as the school librarian at Davenport. While a graduate student, Harry had learned the importance of collaborating with classroom teachers to ensure the relevance of what students learned in the library.

Soon after arriving at Davenport, Harry's principal, Jacqueline Bell, met with him to review his first-year plan for the library. She was impressed with Harry's plans to collaborate with classroom teachers, help both teachers and students learn to use technology for teaching and learning, foster literacy and reading, and provide information literacy skills instruction to all of the students at Davenport. On the first staff day before classes began, Jacqueline introduced Harry to the Davenport faculty and encouraged them to complete Harry's curriculum map, which allowed Harry to plan specific programs, resources, and services to support curriculum-based assignments and projects at the time they are needed.

One of the first projects Harry decided to support was Sally Attridge's fifth grade social studies class. The class assignment was to write research reports about specific countries. According to state and district standards, all middle school students were expected to have learned and applied information literacy skills to a range of research projects. Through his curriculum map, Harry found that Sally was the first teacher to assign a research project at the beginning of the school year.

Harry arranged to meet with Sally initially to identify exactly what Sally expected of her students. During their meeting, Sally said she expected Harry to teach her students how to use the library's resources for their reports and made it very clear that when her students come to the library, they should use printed books and resources for their reports instead of "unreliable and uncontrolled sources from the Internet." She also made sure that Harry knew she had taught sixth grade social studies for almost 25 years, and that because of this, she had an established track record using this method, although she acknowledged that some students seemed somewhat bored with this assignment and some didn't do well on it. Harry was a bit apprehensive about working with Sally because he worried that she saw him as little more than a passive provider of resources, a role chosen by his predecessor at Davenport. Nonetheless, he listened attentively as she described her established ways of preparing students for writing and presenting their reports.

Harry learned that about 65 percent of the students at Davenport spoke English as a second language and had moved to the United States from other countries because many of their parents were either working at the local automobile manufacturing plant or working toward their associate's degree at the nearby community college. Because of this, Sally said many of the students usually wrote their reports about their native countries. Sally told Harry that the students always seemed proud to talk about their native country to the rest of the class, but usually the rest of the class wasn't very interested in paying attention to their classmates' oral presentations of their written reports unless they, too, came from that country. Sally did not like that, but said she never worried about it too much because "at least the students learned a lot about the one country they researched themselves."

Harry was sure there was a better way to work with the students on this assignment. He was skillfully trained and knew that students had access to a variety of individual and collaborative technologies to facilitate and support their research and presentations, providing many more perspectives and much more information than they would ever find in books. He also believed the students should learn—and be interested in learning—about more than just one country, especially because many of the students probably already knew a great deal about their own country.

Extension Questions

1. Should Harry suggest to Sally that there are new and reliable ways for the students to conduct research for their papers?

2. Should Harry develop his own plan for how he envisions the country report, or follow Sally's lead and teach the students as they have been for the past 25 years? Or, is there a third alternative?

References

American Association of School Librarians (AASL). 2007. *Standards for the 21st-Century Learner.* Chicago: American Library Association.

Badke, William. 2009. "Stepping Beyond Wikipedia." *Educational Leadership* 66, no. 6: 54–58.

Bransford, John D., Ann L. Brown, and Rodney R. Cocking. 2000. *How People Learn: Brain, Mind, Experience and School.* Washington, DC: National Academy Press.

Bruner, Jerome. 1986. *Actual Minds, Possible Worlds.* Cambridge, MA: Harvard University Press.

Common Core State Standards Initiative. 2010. "The Standards." National Governors Association Center for Best Practices and Council of Chief State School Officers. http://www.corestandards.org/the-standards.

Conley, David T. 2005. *College Knowledge.* New York: Jossey-Bass.

Costa, Art, and Bena Kallick. 2001. "Project Q. E.: Encouraging Habits of Mind—Phase I." Dr. Stirling McDowell Foundation for Research into Teaching. http://www.mcdowellfoundation.ca/main_mcdowell/projects/research_rep/64_project_qe.pdf.

Deci, Edward, and Richard Flaste. 1995. *Why We Do What We Do: Understanding Self-Motivation.* New York: Penguin.

Deci, E. L., and R. M. Ryan. 1985. *Intrinsic Motivation and Self-Determination in Human Behavior.* New York: Plenum.

Dewey, John. 1938. *Experience and Education.* New York: Simon & Schuster.

Duffy, Thomas M., and Donald J. Cunningham. 1996. "Constructivism: Implications for the Design and Delivery of Instruction." In *Handbook of Research for Educational Communications and Technology,* edited by David Jonassen, 170–198. New York: Macmillan.

International Society for Technology in Education (ISTE). 2007. "ISTE NETS for Students." http://www.iste.org/standards/nets-for-students.aspx.

Jaeger, Michael, and Carol Lauritzen. 1992. "The Construction of Meaning from Experience." National Council of Teachers of English, 82nd National Conference, Louisville, KY, November 18–23.

Keller, John M. 1987. "Development and Use of the ARCS Model of Motivational Design." *Journal of Instructional Development* 10, no. 3 (October): 2–10.

Kuhlthau, Carol C. 1985. *Teaching the Library Research Process.* Metuchen, NJ: Scarecrow Press.

——— 1993. "Implementing a Process Approach to Information Skills: A Study Identifying Indicators of Success in Library Media Programs." *School Library Media Quarterly* 22, no. 1 (Fall): 11–18.

——— 2004. *Seeking Meaning: A Process Approach to Library and Information Services.* Westport, CT: Libraries Unlimited.

McClelland, David C. 1987. *Human Motivation.* Boston: Cambridge University Press.

Meier, Deborah W. 2003. "Becoming Educated: The Power of Ideas." *Principal Leadership* 3, no. 7 (March): 16–19.

New York City School Library System. 2010. *Information Fluency Continuum.* New York City Department of Education. http://schools.nyc.gov/Academics/LibraryServices/StandardsandCurriculum.

Palincsar, Annemarie S. 1998. "Social Constructivist Perspectives on Teaching and Learning." *Annual Review of Psychology*, 49, 345–375.

Pappas, Marjorie L., and Ann E. Tepe. 2002. *Pathways to Knowledge and Inquiry Learning.* Greenwood Village, CO: Teacher Ideas Press.

Partnership for 21st Century Skills. 2003. *Learning for the 21st Century: A Report and Mile Guide for 21st Century Skills.* Washington, DC: Partnership for 21st Century Skills. http://www.21stcenturyskills.org/.

Scardamalia, Marlene, and Carl Bereiter. 1989. "Intentional Learning as a Goal of Instruction." In *Knowing, Learning and Instruction*, edited by Lauren B. Resnick, 361–392. Hillsdale, NJ: Erlbaum.

Small, Ruth V., and Marilyn P. Arnone. 2002. *Make a PACT for Success: Designing Effective Information Presentations.* Lanham, MD: Scarecrow Press.

———— and Myke Gluck. 1994. "The Relationship of Motivational Conditions to Effective Instructional Attributes: A Magnitude Scaling Approach." *Educational Technology* 34, no. 8 (October): 33–40.

Steinberg, L. 1996. *Beyond the Classroom: Why School Reform Has Failed and What Parents Need to Do.* New York: Touchstone.

Stipek, Deborah, and Denise H. Daniels. 1988. "Declining Perceptions of Competence: A Consequence of Changes in the Child or in the Educational Environment?" *Journal of Educational Psychology* 80, no. 3 (September): 352–356.

Stripling, Barbara K. 2003. "Inquiry-Based Learning." In *Curriculum Connections through the Library*, edited by B. K. Stripling, and S. Hughes-Hassell, 3–39. Westport, CT: Libraries Unlimited.

Stripling, Barbara K. 2008. "Dispositions: Getting Beyond 'Whatever.'" *School Library Media Activities Monthly* 25, no. 2 (October): 47–50.

Venkatesh, Murali, Ruth Small, and Janet Marsden. 2003. *Learning in Community: Reflections on Practice.* Norwell, MA: Kluwer Academic.

Vroom, Victor. 1994. *Work and Motivation.* Hoboken, NJ: John Wiley & Sons.

Vygotsky, Lev. 1978. *The Mind in Society: The Development of Higher Psychological Processes.* Cambridge, MA: Harvard University Press.

DIGGING DEEPER

Deci, Edward L., Richard Koestner, and Richard M. Ryan. 2001. "Extrinsic Rewards and Intrinsic Motivation in Education: Reconsidered Once Again." *Review of Educational Research* 71, no. 1 (Spring): 1–27.

Kuhlthau, Carol C., Leslie K. Manietes, and Ann K. Caspari. 2007. *Guided Inquiry: Learning in the 21st Century.* Westport, CT: Libraries Unlimited.

Marlowe, Bruce, and Marilyn Page. 1998. *Creating and Sustaining the Constructivist Classroom.* Thousand Oaks, CA: Corwin Press.

Pressley, M., Karen R. Harris, and M. B. Marks. 1992. "But Good Strategy Instructors are Constructivists!" *Educational Psychology Review* 4, 3–31.

Stripling, Barbara. 2007. "Assessing Information Fluency: Gathering Evidence of Student Learning." *School Library Media Activities Monthly* 23 (April): 25–29.

Stripling, Barbara K. 2007. "Teaching for Understanding." In *School Reform and the School Library Media Specialist*, edited by Sandra Hughes-Hassell and Violet H. Harada, 37–55. Westport, CT: Libraries Unlimited.

———— 2009. "Teaching Inquiry with Primary Sources." *Teaching with Primary Sources Quarterly* (Summer): 2–4. http://www.loc.gov/teachers/tps/quarterly/0907/pdf/TPSQuarterlySummer09.pdf.

White, R. W. 1959. "Motivation Reconsidered: The Concept of Competence." *Psychological Review* 66, no. 5: 297–333.

Purpose: Beginning at the End

The library doors swung open and in dashed four fifth grade students eager to get started on their research project. "Hello Mrs. Jameson," they said almost in unison. Then, Mary continued, "Mr. Briggs told us we should come to the library and find information for our project. The four of us are researching fossils." Mrs. Jameson asked what kind of information they were looking for. "Just stuff on fossils," said Daniel. After querying the students for less than a minute or so, it quickly became obvious that the students were not very clear about the overall purpose of the assignment. Mrs. Jameson had her work cut out for her.

Introduction

If you were to ask students coming to your library to explain the purpose of their assignment, that is, what the specific task is and what they will learn from it, some of them will have no idea. Jere Brophy, a noted researcher on motivation and learning from Michigan State University, found that less than 2 percent of the elementary teachers he observed explained the purpose of the assignment to students (Stipek and Seal, 2002). What is even more astounding is that 8 percent of the time, teachers stated they didn't expect students to enjoy or to do well on the assignment! Does this sound like a self-fulfilling prophecy to you?

This part of the process is like creating a "road map" to learning and motivation. So let's start with a question that lies at the heart of this chapter. We will call it the essential question.

Essential Question

- How does having a clear purpose improve inquiry-based instruction?

The essential question will help frame the rest of the chapter. As mentioned in Chapter 1, defining the purpose of your instruction entails determining why instruction is needed and what outcomes you expect from students. Here are desired outcomes for readers related to Chapter 2.

Chapter Outcomes and Indicators

By the end of this chapter and by taking advantage of this book's companion website (http://teachingforinquiry.net), you should be able to achieve the following learning outcomes and indicators:

1. OUTCOME: Understand the relationship between needs assessment and a backward design approach to planning effective instruction.
   a. INDICATOR: Identify and describe at least two methods for conducting an instructional needs assessment.
   b. INDICATOR: Use a backward design approach to develop essential questions for a unit, learning outcomes, and indicators, benchmarks, and motivational goals for a lesson.
2. OUTCOME: Use AASL's *Standards for the 21st-Century Learner* as a guideline for planning and organizing your instructional plans.
   a. INDICATOR: Understand the organizational structure of the Standards and its relationship to defining the purpose of instruction.
   b. INDICATOR: Use the Standards to plan what you will teach and how you will assess student learning.
3. OUTCOME: Gain knowledge and skills in other areas of importance to defining purpose.
   a. INDICATOR: Categorize observed cognitive learning activities according to their Bloom's Taxonomy level.
   b. INDICATOR: Suggest at least two ways to assess learning outcomes and indicators.
   c. INDICATOR: Identify at least three constraints or barriers that might be an obstacle to learning success.

Getting Started

How can you determine your route, what you might need along the way, and whether you have reached your intended destination, unless you have clearly identified your starting location, where you want to go, and why? In other words, how will you know you got there if you don't know where you're going?

So, the first step in this process is to define your purpose by (1) determining your instructional needs (curriculum, students' knowledge needs, etc.), (2) identifying the big ideas or essential questions that frame the instruction, (3) clearly articulating what learning outcomes you hope to achieve and what indicators and benchmarks you will use to assess whether those outcomes have been achieved and, last but not least, (4) identifying your motivational goals.

You will soon discover that doing a good job of defining your purpose will greatly influence the effectiveness of the content and techniques you select and use in your instruction.

Needs Assessment

The first step in determining instructional needs is deciding if instruction is needed at all. This step (determining exactly what instruction is needed and who needs it) should not be done in isolation but in consultation with classroom teachers and integrated with the curriculum, classroom instruction, homework assignments, and/or class projects. Teaching a skill to students who already have mastered it or creating a lesson that is clearly beyond the scope of the prescribed curriculum will likely be perceived as having dubious value and may not be the best use of your time.

Providing a Rationale for Your Instruction

Conducting a formal needs assessment is one way to gain a clear understanding of what specific instruction is needed and for whom. This step should occur *before* designing and developing instruction. For example, you could review established curriculum for each subject area to determine which digital and information literacy concepts and skills should be taught for each subject area, at each grade level, and when. Or, you could make up a survey for classroom teachers designed to let you know what topics are covered and when so that you can create a curriculum map, tailor your instruction to students' learning needs, and allow collaborative lesson planning efforts. All of this information can be considered part of your overall evidence-based practice to gather "meaningful and systematic evidence on dimensions of teaching and learning that matter to the school and its support community" (Todd, 2003: Slide 5).

You could develop an assessment instrument to determine what twenty-first-century learning goals students have or have not mastered. If you would prefer to not use a test of skills, you could opt to collect information on students' perceived competence in one or more areas. You could frame this assessment as something that will help you plan future instruction, making sure students understand that it is not graded. One instrument with excellent reliability and validity is the Perceived Competence in Information Skills Scale (Arnone, Small, and Reynolds, 2010) used in a study of more than 1,200 students nationally (we include this measure in Appendix 1). Another assessment method to consider is designing an interview protocol and then interviewing key teachers about their perceptions of what students know or need to learn, for what purpose and when. This information can be placed into a spreadsheet to create a curriculum map. A curriculum map is an essential tool for identifying the library and information services and resources needed throughout the school year. Or, you could use a combination of any or all of these methods to assess the needs of your learning audience.

While all of these methods are highly recommended as means for obtaining an overall, broad picture of learning needs in your school related to successful library research, they are fairly costly in time and effort. You may also want to use some faster and more targeted (and less formal) methods for determining the instructional needs in your school (e.g., conversations with students, discussions with teachers) so that you can deliver library instruction "just in time," when it is needed, rather than "just in case" it is needed. As you can see, by seeking information from other educators within your school, you have already initiated collaborative planning. You will find some useful tips for collaboration later in this chapter.

> **STOP! THINK! DO!**
>
> What are some proactive ways to determine whether, where, when, and with whom information skills instruction is needed in your school? Brainstorm at least three ways you plan to seek out this information.

Following your initial collaborative meeting, you should have a pretty good idea about where and for whom the need exists for twenty-first-century skills instruction. From instructional needs assessment, we can now move on to the actual design stage of lesson planning. With all the information you have collected, where do you start to put it all together?

Types of Learning Goals

Also critical to defining the purpose of your instruction is a clear understanding of the different types of learning goals. This requires an awareness of the levels of learning in the cognitive domain, as described by Bloom (1956).

Levels of Learning

Benjamin Bloom and his colleagues at the University of Chicago developed a taxonomy that provides a classification of levels of cognitive goals, knowledge acquisition, and the development of intellectual abilities and skills (Bloom, 1956). Bloom's Taxonomy identifies a range of mental processes, from memorization to the ability to think and solve problems. (Note: There are also taxonomies for the affective [Krathwohl, Bloom, and Masia, 1964] and psychomotor [Harrow, 1972] domains. For more information on these taxonomies, see "Digging Deeper" at the end of this chapter.)

Bloom's Taxonomy serves as a way to categorize learning goals and questions, allowing design of instruction that matches learning objectives to the content presented and to the assessment questions asked. Bloom and his associates identified six cognitive levels, ordered by complexity (see Figure 2.1). The lowest cognitive level is *knowledge*-level learning, which includes recall and recognition of information. For example, presenting a range of information literacy skills and requiring students to list them from memory is an example of knowledge-level learning.

The next higher level is the *comprehension* level. At this level, students are expected to understand the meaning of content presented. For example, asking students to explain the meaning of information literacy in their own words (as opposed to verbatim in knowledge-level learning) is comprehension-level learning. Both knowledge and comprehension are considered lower-level cognitive skills.

If you want your students to be able to apply the information presented to new situations, you would be requiring them to learn on the *application* level. If you demonstrate to students how to use a database by performing a search on that database and then ask them to apply their learning to a new search, they would be demonstrating application-level learning. This level requires higher-order thinking skills from your students.

The final three cognitive levels are considered the highest cognitive levels, those required for critical thinking and problem-solving tasks, the building blocks of twenty-first-century learning. The first of these is the analysis level of learning. At the *analysis* level, students are expected to be able to break down a problem into its component parts, examine each part, and use this information to develop conclusions or make inferences. The ability to categorize books by genre is an example of analysis-level learning.

Learning on the *synthesis* level requires the learner to take prior knowledge and/or new information and fit them together in a new and useful way. For example, once students have taken notes from their information sources, writing a research paper that incorporates their notes with their own ideas in a new and creative way can be considered a synthesis-level activity.

Making judgments about the value of materials or ideas is learning at the *evaluation* level. When students must decide which information resources are most appropriate to help them solve their information problem or deciding which twentieth-century American author's work is highest in literary quality, these are examples of activities requiring evaluation-level thinking. Figure 2.1 summarizes the cognitive levels according to Bloom's Taxonomy (Bloom, 1956).

More recently, Anderson and Krathwohl (2001) reconsidered the order of some of the cognitive levels and revised Bloom's original taxonomy of the cognitive domain. They replaced nouns with verbs and reordered the final two levels, ranking the creative thinking process (formerly called "synthesis") as the highest cognitive level. Inquiry-based learning requires these highest levels of cognition. The revised version of the taxonomy with examples of actions appears in

Table 2.1 (Anderson and Krathwohl, 2001). The sample actions that refer to the new taxonomy are helpful in creating benchmarks for student learning.

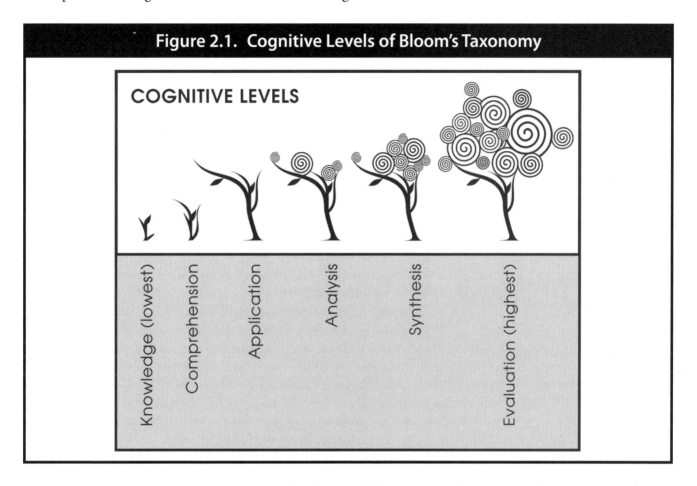

Figure 2.1. Cognitive Levels of Bloom's Taxonomy

Table 2.1. Cognitive Levels for Revised Taxonomy	
Cognitive Level Revised (former)	**Sample Actions**
Remember (Knowledge)	Recalls, recognizes, defines, describes, identifies, lists, matches, outlines, states, labels, quotes, names
Comprehend (Comprehension)	Translates, exemplifies, classifies, compares, summarizes, infers, explains, understands, generalizes, interprets, describes, paraphrases
Apply (Application)	Applies, demonstrates, manipulates, modifies, relates, shows, solves, uses, changes, executes, implements
Analyze (Analysis)	Compares, contrasts, diagrams, deconstructs, differentiates, separates, selects, infers, organizes, attributes
Evaluate (Evaluation)	Appraises, concludes, criticizes, critiques, evaluates, judges, justifies, summarizes, supports, assesses, ranks, monitors
Create (Synthesis)	Combines, compiles, composes, creates, generates, revises, integrates, formulates, plans, produces

The 21st-Century Skills for Learning are generally higher-order processes and therefore require divergent knowledge and skills (such as classifying, organizing, analyzing, and critiquing) for critical thinking and problem-solving exercises and activities. Therefore, library and information skills instruction that focuses mainly on lower-level cognitive activities such as memorization and fact-finding should be used sparingly and only when appropriate (e.g., remembering how to sign out a library book using the online circulation scanning system).

Matching Content Expectations to Skills

A team of preservice librarians from New York City, Miriam Pinero, Gwynn White, and Lisette Felipe-Rossi worked together to develop a unit plan on Tropical Rainforests for grades 3–5. The goals of this unit are to (1) engage students, individually and cooperatively, in active learning about the rainforests and to develop students' skills in research and presentation, (2) allow students to learn in-depth about tropical rainforests and their levels, products of the rainforest, indigenous societies, and deforestation, and (3) foster cooperative learning among students by sharing their learning with classmates, enhancing the breadth of knowledge for the group. (This unit can be found in its entirety in *S.O.S. for Information Literacy*, http://www.informationliteracy.org.)

> **TAKING ACTION**
>
> Using the matrix in Table 2.2, can you think of one or two ways that you could bring in the Standards for the 21st-Century Learner Goals?

The unit addresses subjects from the Science (plants and animals, weather, ecosystems), English Language Arts (reading, writing) and Social Studies (geography, people, and cultures) curricula. The team used Anderson and Krathwohl's (2001) revised taxonomy to create a content-performance matrix of learning types for their unit (see Table 2.2). The matrix is driven by subject area content, not library-related skills. It provides librarians with a basic understanding of what content would be taught so that they could then determine which library skills to teach in the context of the subject area content.

Forming Purpose of Inquiry-Based Instruction around the *Standards for the 21st-Century Learner*

For an in-depth breakdown of all the indicators and benchmarks related to the standards, we suggest you consult the publications *Standards for the 21st-Century Learner* (AASL, 2007) and *Standards for the 21st-Century Learner in Action* (AASL, 2009) and refer to them often as you proceed through the instructional design process. These publications provide complete knowledge of the standards and offer many useful action examples. Notice that just below each action example presented in the text (AASL, 2009: 68–114) the header is labeled "Standards for the 21st-Century Learner Goals." Placing the word "Goals" above the table that includes the standard and strands, indicators, and benchmarks suggests that the term Goals is an umbrella, all-encompassing term.

The Evolution of the Standards

The current AASL standards differ from previous standards in two important ways: (1) they recognize the importance of technology in today's world and (2) inquiry-based teaching and learning are underlying common beliefs. They also acknowledge that information literacy is

	Table 2.2. Content-Performance Matrix of Learning Levels						
Goal No.	Content	Remember	Understand	Apply	Analyze	Evaluate	Create
#1	The student will identify the locations of the tropical rainforests.	X					
#2	The student will illustrate the levels of the rainforest.		X				
#3	The student will utilize rainforest products to reinforce how they affect our daily lives.			X			
#4	The student will distinguish between the different indigenous societies of the rainforest.				X		
#5	The student will evaluate the importance of the rainforest and generate a critique on the effects of deforestation.					X	
#6	The student will make a mini rainforest.						X

one of multiple literacies (e.g., digital, visual, and media literacies) necessary for student success. The contribution of motivation and affect to learning is emphasized through inclusion of dispositions in action; further discussion of dispositions in more detail is found in the motivation section of this chapter. The standards place particular emphasis on collaboration between librarians and classroom teachers as a key to success for student achievement. (Some tips for successful collaboration are highlighted later in this chapter.)

Structure of Standards and Their Relationship to Defining the Purpose of Instruction

Referring to the organizational structure of the *Standards for the 21st-Century Learner*, you will see that they include four top-level standards that are presented in very broad terms covering several areas of critical importance to learners from academic learning to learning for one's personal pursuits of knowledge and interests. The top level standards follow:

1. Inquire, think critically, and gain knowledge
2. Draw conclusions, make informed decisions, apply knowledge to new situations, and create new knowledge
3. Share knowledge and participate ethically and productively as members of a democratic society, and
4. Pursue personal and aesthetic growth (AASL, 2009: 7)

Since they are at the top level, each could be considered as a learning destination, a final outcome, or the established goals. For example, that students are able to use their skills, resources, and tools to "draw conclusions, make informed decisions, apply knowledge to new situations, and create new knowledge (Standard 2)" represents the desired outcome or goal. (Be sure to think about how these top-level standards are related to both backward design and outcome-based evaluation, discussed later in this chapter.)

These standards are then delineated into four categories, or strands, ensuring that student needs beyond academics are considered. The strands included under each standard are skills, dispositions, responsibilities, and self-assessment strategies.

To be useful in an educational context, learner outcomes/goals must be fine-tuned to cover the range of actions that might demonstrate achievement of the standard. AASL uses the term indicators to determine achievement of an outcome. Indicators are found beneath each strand in the Standards. They tell someone reading your instructional plan how students might display the competencies related to each standard. For example, one indicator under Standard 1 is "[Students can] use prior and background knowledge as context for new learning" (1.1.2). The numbering system refers to Standard 1 under the first category (Skills) referring to the second indicator or 1.1.2.

While indicators within the standards provide additional information about what types of performance can demonstrate competence, they do not indicate for what audience (grade level) or what specifically the learner should be able to do that is age appropriate. That is why AASL suggests benchmarks for the skills category of the Standards. Here is the benchmark for Standard 1.1.2 for grade 5: *With guidance generate a list of keywords for an inquiry-based project.*

The benchmarks for the Skills strand of the Standards come closest to what was once referred to as *learning objectives*. Using the ABCD method for creating learning objectives, you would specify the Audience (e.g., fifth grade students), Behavior (e.g., generate a list of keywords), Condition (e.g., with guidance from the librarian) and Degree. Degree refers to the level of success needed to accomplish the objective such as the number or appropriateness of the generated keywords. In the previous benchmark example, the degree is left to the discretion of the educator. In the revised lesson-planning template presented in this book, the word *objectives* is replaced by the word *benchmark*, so applying the ABCD formula remains the same. The benchmark should specify who will do the learning, what learning will occur, under what conditions, and the degree of success required. Let's look at one more example of a benchmark: *Using two types of search strategies, ninth grade students will locate five resources needed for their research assignment.*

For this benchmark, "Using two types of search strategies" specifies the condition, "ninth grade students" identifies the learning audience, and "locate five resources needed for their research assignment" specifies what learning behavior is expected and how many resources are needed to demonstrate competence (i.e., the degree). In addition to benchmarks provided in the Standards, you can find benchmarks for every grade range in the continuum of inquiry skills for K–12 using the *New York City Inquiry Benchmark Skills* (see Table 4.1, p. 72, in Chapter 4).

Translating Skills Benchmarks into Assessments and Criteria

If you have done a good job creating benchmarks that demonstrate grade-appropriate learning for each standard addressed, it is easy to create your assessments. Assessments should accurately reflect written benchmarks; for example, the assessment for the benchmark listed earlier (i.e.,

Using two types of search strategies, ninth grade students will locate five resources needed for their research assignment) should include a mechanism by which students can actually demonstrate achievement of the benchmark.

Once goals for instruction are established, consider how to assess whether you and your students have successfully reached your destination; i.e., whether, by the end of instruction, Standards for the 21st-Century Learner Goals have been successfully achieved. It is never too early to begin thinking about and planning an assessment strategy. You'll also need to think about ways to collect and measure the data.

> **STOP! THINK! DO!**
>
> What assessment methods might be most appropriate for measuring competence related to the benchmark?

There are a number of ways to assess whether instructional goals have been attained. Of course, traditional paper-and-pencil tests can be used, but librarians often prefer to look for alternative ways to assess achievement of selected standards, such as rubrics, projects, and portfolios.

Assessment is typically associated with the end of the learning process, but, actually, some type of assessment should be conducted at various points during the lesson. You might assess (or students could self-assess) learning to that point or of a single concept or skill presented. Using frequent, brief assessments throughout a lesson will allow catching and addressing any learning problems before they become too deeply rooted and more difficult to undo or reverse. In their information literacy model, Stripling and Pitts (1988) demonstrated the importance of frequent assessment by building in reflection points where students are required to stop and self-assess their personal learning progress.

Assessment of any kind requires feedback to students. When you provide informative feedback, it allows students to know where they have succeeded and where (and how) they can improve. It provides the fuel for student learning growth and development. The motivational feedback you provide encourages students' performance and effort, helps students feel good about what they have already accomplished, and stimulates the continued effort to learn. We will discuss motivation assessment in more detail later in the chapter.

Unfortunately, assessment is one part of the process that is often given little attention or even may be overlooked by librarians when planning their instruction. Most librarians are not required to grade students' work or provide other formal assessments, therefore some look to the classroom teacher to assume that responsibility. However, student learning and motivation are affected when those responsible for instruction fail to do any assessment and provide feedback. Assessment can be as informal as observing students performing a task or asking questions to determine what students know and then providing feedback on the quality of their performance. This also helps to establish your credibility as an instructor and instructional collaborator.

In Chapter 5, the topic of assessment will be addressed in more detail, including numerous techniques that can be used. Thinking about it now, in relation to defining the purpose of your instruction and selecting the relevant standards, indicators, and benchmarks, can facilitate the process down the road.

Beginning at the End

Beginning at the end simply means that you need to first identify the desired learning (goals) that you wish to occur as a result of instruction and the evidence you will need to collect to determine the degree of success attained by students. Once accomplished, planning the activities and procedures that are required in order to achieve those results becomes much easier. This approach is sometimes referred to as *backward design*.

Backward Design

In *Understanding by Design* (Wiggins and McTighe, 2005), the authors stress the dangers of activity-focused design in which the teacher-designed activities are the driving force, as opposed to staying true to the big ideas or essential questions that provide the continuity of an overall unit or curriculum plan. Instead, Wiggins and McTighe suggest using a backward design approach that focuses first on establishing the desired results for students (goals in terms of standards to be achieved) and subsequently, the activities and the particular facts and concepts to be learned. Without the bigger picture, it is difficult to make learning facts, concepts, and principles meaningful or relevant. The big ideas and essential questions provide the weaving threads and glue that hold a unit together. (We'll return to the subject of essential questions a bit later in this chapter.)

Backward design involves three stages: (1) identify desired results, (2) determine acceptable evidence, and (3) plan learning experiences and instruction. As you proceed throughout this chapter, you will see that establishing the purpose of your lesson involves the first two stages, and that once defined, the actual lesson planning builds on this initial effort.

Outcome-Based Evaluation

Another similar approach to backward design used in education is called *outcome-based evaluation* (OBE). In fact, it is almost impossible to apply for education grants these days without a solid outcome-based evaluation plan. Applied to the design of an instructional unit, for example, outcome-based evaluation is a systematic way to assess the extent to which instruction and related activities have achieved the desired learning results for students. Thus, similar to Wiggins and McTighe's (1988) backward design approach, outcome-based evaluation begins at the end by identifying the desired learning outcomes up-front (based, of course, on having established the need for instruction already) and then specifying indicators that are more specific and measurable.

Desired outcomes are changes in learners as a result of instructional intervention. These changes can be in the form of improved skills and abilities, attitudes or motivation, knowledge, or some behavior. While outcomes are generally stated in broad terms (just like goals in backward design), indicators (that the outcomes have been achieved) are more conducive to measurement. Outcomes may be thought of as your road map's destination while indicators provide your journey's landmarks along the way. Arriving at these landmarks should be moderately challenging, making students stretch yet keeping learning success within their reach. Through assessment, they also provide evidence of your success in reaching the intended destination through thoughtful, thorough instructional planning. These differences will become clearer as we move through this chapter.

OBE also includes making note of the inputs needed to achieve results. Applied to education and lesson planning in particular, these inputs are the resources and materials that you will need to present the unit and lessons. Once all of this has been defined, the activities that will most likely lead to the intended results are planned and developed. However, attempting to create instructional activities before defining the clear purpose of instruction is like putting the cart before the horse; therefore, arriving at your intended destination becomes much less likely. By focusing on purpose, this chapter provides the foundation needed to improve inquiry-based instruction to get the desired results. The design of specific content and activities to achieve your purpose is the focus of later chapters.

At the end of this chapter you will find some suggested resources for learning more about outcome-based evaluation and backward design. By understanding the value of these approaches, you are more likely to develop clarity, insight, and a level of comfort with lesson planning. In the next section of this chapter, you will discover that the structure of AASL's *Standards for the 21st-Century Learner* is very conducive to implementing such approaches in planning inquiry-based instruction.

Integration of Content and Skills

Keep in mind that while your job as a librarian is to develop instruction based on the *Standards for the 21st-Century Learner*, they must be taught in the context of the curriculum. So, the lesson planning template we present in this book complements AASL's layout and requires you to make that connection right up front. We have chosen to focus on a template for *lesson* planning (rather than *unit* planning, for example), as it is the most epitomizing form of instructional planning.

In your front-end assessment, you should have garnered information about the content area knowledge required by the curriculum. You can access a compendium of national content standards developed by the Mid-Continent Research for Education and Learning at http://www.mcrel.org/standards-benchmarks/. You can also go online to locate the grade level breakdown for content standards, state by state, or access the Common Core State Standards at http://www.corestandards.org/the-standards.

> **CHECKPOINT**
>
> At this point, we have discussed backward design and outcome-based evaluation planning as critical to defining the purpose of instruction. We also have described how the structure of the *Standards for the 21st-Century Learner* is conducive to these approaches and to clearly defining the purpose of inquiry-based instruction. Now we move on to the Lesson Planning template and more ideas for planning instruction.

Lesson Planning and Template

Essential Questions

When co-planning a unit with the classroom teacher, your plan should include the essential questions that guide the planning process. Often these essential questions refer to those that the classroom teacher must cover from a content perspective, but they should also trigger ideas for how you can integrate twenty-first-century learner goals into specific lesson plans. To provide meaning and context for students, it is imperative that you relate each lesson plan back to these essential question(s) of the overall unit.

Figure 2.2 is an example of a brief overview of a unit by librarian Bonnie French that starts with an essential or big question/idea and tells just enough in the overview to get her principal excited. You can also find this unit in the *S.O.S. for Information Literacy* database at http://www.informationliteracy.org.

As you begin the planning process, use the Lesson Planning Template (see Appendix 2) to help create your lesson plan. Through collaboration efforts with other educators and using the information you have gathered related to the twenty-first-century learning skills and dispositions

Figure 2.2. Overview of Unit: Polar Animals Graphic

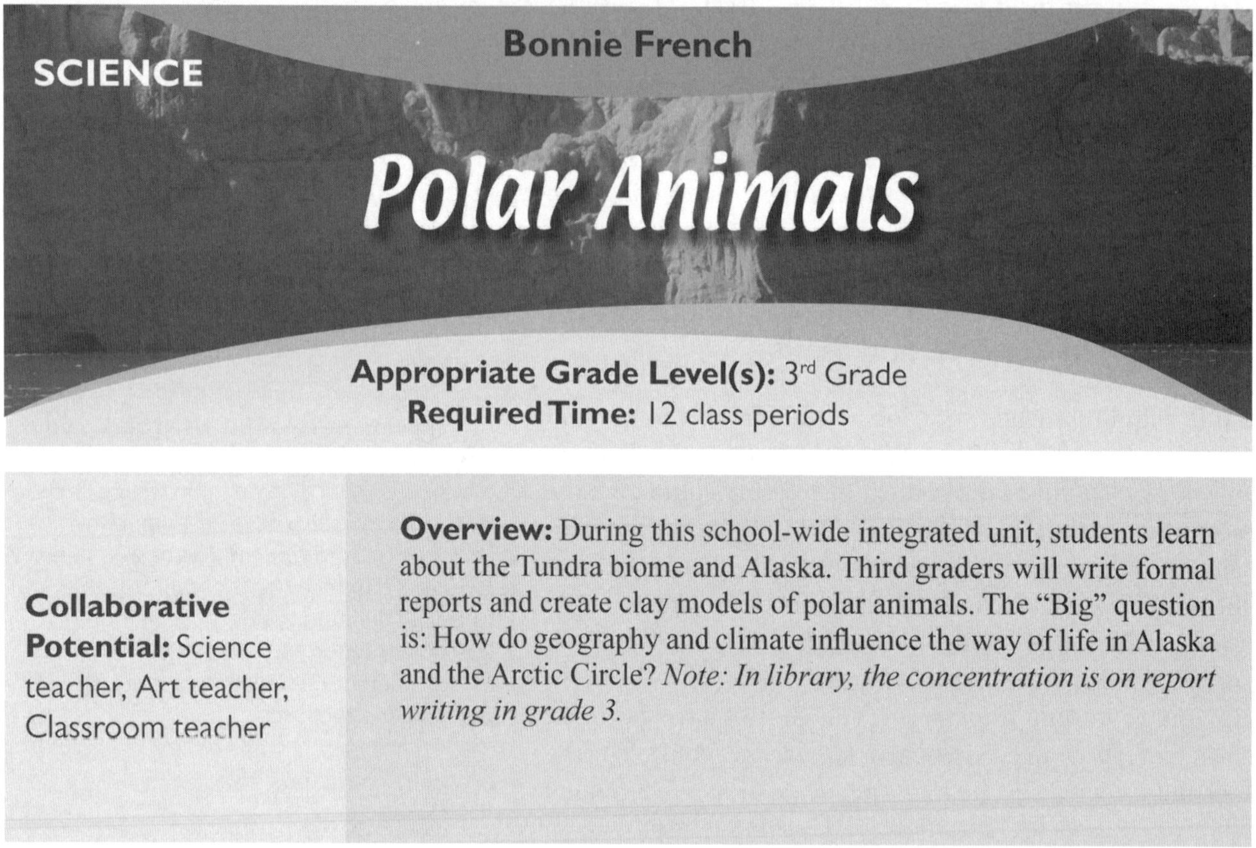

SCIENCE

Bonnie French

Polar Animals

Appropriate Grade Level(s): 3rd Grade
Required Time: 12 class periods

Collaborative Potential: Science teacher, Art teacher, Classroom teacher

Overview: During this school-wide integrated unit, students learn about the Tundra biome and Alaska. Third graders will write formal reports and create clay models of polar animals. The "Big" question is: How do geography and climate influence the way of life in Alaska and the Arctic Circle? *Note: In library, the concentration is on report writing in grade 3.*

Source: Arnone, Small, and Stripling, 2010. Used by permission of the authors.

that need to be addressed in your school, you may already have what is needed to complete several elements of the lesson plan (see Figure 2.3). Think of a descriptive (and motivating) title, provide the grade level and estimated required time, and choose the context for instruction in the library, that is, whether your lesson is a single stand-alone lesson or one of multiple lessons in a unit, etc. From the initial planning session, you should be able to gauge the collaborative potential of the lesson plan or unit. Ideally, you should strive for a high degree of collaboration; we'll discuss more about collaboration later. The classroom teacher will provide the content topic and scope; you will later select relevant Standards for the 21st-Century Learner Goals that you can address within the context of that topic.

In the overview section of the lesson-planning template, you can describe the larger unit and essential questions that help frame the individual lesson plan. You can also briefly describe the specific lesson plan that you are presenting. Providing this information is helpful if you plan on sharing the lesson plan with a colleague or your principal; they will know exactly what your lesson plan is about and hopefully they will be excited about it. Take a look at the lesson-planning template for all the aspects that we just discussed. The complete template (includes fields for connection to state/local standards, AASL Standards, Motivational Goals, Assessment and Criteria, Instructional Activities, and more) is in Appendix 2 of this book and an electronic printable form may be found on the companion website (http://teachingforinquiry.net).

Figure 2.3. Lesson Plan Template Graphic

Teaching Inquiry: Engaging the Learner Within
Lesson Planning Template

GENERAL INFORMATION

Librarian:

Lesson Plan/Unit Title:

Appropriate Grade Level(s):   **Required Time:**

Library Context: (Check one below)

☐ Fixed   ☐ Flexible   ☐ Combination   ☐ Individualized Instruction

☐ Stand-alone lesson   ☐ Lesson in a unit   ☐ Multiple lessons in a unit

Collaboration Potential: ☐ None   ☐ Limited   ☐ Moderate   ☐ Intensive

Overview:

Content Topic(s):

Collaboration: Key to Success

Hopefully, you already use collaboration as a way to determine students' learning needs. In its 1990 report, the Holmes Group (1990) cited collaboration as one of the five essential elements of all educators' core knowledge. Research reveals that students have a greater opportunity for successful learning if the teacher and librarian collaborate and plan together when integrating information literacy skills and subject matter (Pitts, 1995; Todd, 1995; Lance, 2002). Gross and Kientz conclude that "collaborating with teachers is the only way to ensure that information literacy skills will be learned within a meaningful context" (Gross and Kientz, 1999: 24). This reinforces the importance of librarian-teacher collaboration for teaching information skills, for example, in the context of relevant curriculum and standards.

Collaboration requires a shared vision among the collaborative partners. These types of synergistic interactions and shared decision-making experiences often lead to more creative and effective instruction than would have occurred with librarians and teachers working independently. In fact, collaborative lesson planning is often highly motivating for the collaborators themselves. The relationships formed through collaborative lesson planning and delivery assure a stronger educational environment for everyone involved.

Collaboration was discussed earlier as a critical component of your needs assessment process. How do you encourage successful collaborations? Here are some helpful tips.

Top 10 Tips for Successful Collaboration

1. **Serve refreshments.** Food is a great motivator! Anytime you want teachers to come to your library to collaborate (or for any other reason), serve refreshments. If you serve it, they will come.

2. **Develop a "collaborative mentality."** This means keeping your collaboration "antennae" at full extension, seeking out collaboration opportunities wherever and whenever they arise.

3. **Establish credibility.** Get "up close and personal" with the curricula and curriculum standards for each grade level in your school and determine the most likely "payoff points," where you can immediately provide instructional services and learning resources to meet the needs of both teachers and students. Be able to "talk the talk" during your collaborative interactions by reading education journals and seeking other important, relevant information about the most current topics related to instruction and learning.

4. **If you are new to collaboration, don't try to collaborate with everyone at once.** Instead, start with one classroom or special area teacher who has expressed interest in integrating information skills into the curriculum or in finding more/new ways to work with you. Develop a track record and document it.

5. **Share stories of successful collaborations.** Make sure your principal and the other teachers are aware of your collaborative activities by talking about them at faculty meetings, in your library's website or newsletter, and/or in reports. This also benefits the teacher with whom you are collaborating.

6. **Go to them.** Hang out with teachers; have lunch in the teachers' room, go to team planning meetings, join curriculum and technology committees—whatever it takes to be able to learn and understand what's important to them and their students.

7. **Be enthusiastic, approachable, and a good listener.** These traits will go a long way in fostering a motivation to collaborate. No one enjoys collaborating with someone who clearly doesn't care, is distant, or who only likes the sound of his or her own voice. While being proactive is a must, I often advise first-year librarians to "keep their eyes and ears open and their mouths shut" at least for the first few weeks of the school year. Of course, we don't mean this literally but it's important, when you are new to a school, to do a lot of observing and listening, getting to know who the leaders are on your faculty, who your most likely supporters will be and, even more important, who the most likely resisters will be to your collaboration efforts. Observe whether and in what ways your school demonstrates a "collaborative culture" in which people work together in various

ways toward common goals for the benefit of students. Above all, listen to what people are saying to you and to each other. As Bush (2003: 7) states, "It is when we actively listen to each other that transformation of thought occurs." Armed with this information, you can then seek out those leaders and supporters for initial collaboration. Believe us; human nature dictates that others will follow. While you may not convince all the classroom teachers in your school to collaborate, you will likely persuade a majority of them over time.

8. **Know your stuff!** Be an expert in what librarians know and can do that classroom teachers can't/don't; this will make you invaluable to your teacher colleagues. You bring essential knowledge to the collaboration table—you are the expert on information literacy skills, resources, and technologies and how to integrate them with classroom instruction.

9. **Ensure value and an expectation for success.** Make sure your collaborator(s) clearly see there is value in collaboration for both of you (and the students) and that you each have the knowledge and skills necessary to be successful collaborative partners.

10. **Don't assume knowledge.** You'll find that at least some teachers (and even your principal) won't know much about information literacy or why it is important or about some of the new technologies and how to best use them. When first meeting with classroom teachers, don't use library, technology, or information literacy jargon unless you are sure they understand it. Try to find ways to share this information with them in a way that makes them feel excited and empowered to be part of the process, rather than embarrassed or afraid to be involved in something they don't understand. Start with terms that classroom teachers use and understand and then begin to bring in more technical terms, clearly explaining what they mean. For example, rather than talking about the use of technologies that provide bibliographic control, simply explain that when they or their students use online catalogs and databases, these tools have built-in ways for them to find the information they are looking for quickly and easily. (Small, 2005: 36–37)

> **CHECKPOINT**
>
> You have come a long way since the last checkpoint! Already, you have seen all the sections of the lesson planning template that relate to the purpose of your lesson plan. We've discussed how essential questions can frame a unit. You have read about different types of learning and have seen the difference between the original Bloom's Taxonomy and the newer revised version. Finally, we've shared some helpful tips on forging successful collaborative relationships. In the next section, you'll discover that as educators, we must also address learner motivation as we plan and define the purpose of instruction.

Collaboration requires time and perhaps several planning sessions. Part of this time is devoted to proving credibility as an instructional partner and part is in the actual collaboration, creating and then rethinking your instructional design. As you become more experienced and work more with a particular teacher or teachers, the less you will have to do the former and the more the latter process will go more quickly and smoothly.

Student Motivation

The Motivation Overlay to Instruction

Your students do more than just learn during a lesson. They also form attitudes and develop values toward learning in general, toward the content you are teaching, and toward you as an instructor. These are important to consider because they can affect the content you select and the teaching techniques (and assessment measures) that you use in your lesson. They also affect whether your lesson will result in your students becoming engaged in the learning process and developing an intellectual curiosity, an intrinsic motivation to learn, and a lifelong love of learning. Specifically, they also do the following:

- Generate excitement for learning a range of twenty-first-century learning skills.
- Foster a belief that learning these skills is important and useful for reaching current and future learning goals.
- Build students' self-confidence so that they believe they can learn and apply these skills in a variety of contexts (both learning and personal).
- Help students feel good about their learning successes so they will want to experience more of them.

We refer to these feelings as motivational goals for instruction.

Research conducted by Small in 1999 explored how K–8 librarians motivated students to learn information literacy skills. Based largely on the research of Carol Kuhlthau (1989; 1993) that identified specific feelings that students had as they proceeded through the research process and John Keller's (1987) ARCS (Attention, Relevance, Confidence, Satisfaction) Model of Motivational Design, which prescribes specific motivational strategies to address specific motivational problems, the research revealed that librarians used a large number of strategies to gain and maintain student attention and interest, but very few strategies that provided relevance, built confidence, and promoted learning satisfaction.

As a result of this research and based on the previous work of both Kuhlthau and Keller, Small and Arnone (2000) developed the Motivation Overlay for Information Literacy Skills Instruction, which provides a motivational framework for teaching information literacy skills that can be superimposed on any information skills model. The Motivation Overlay lists nine general motivational goals that are categorized by a time frame of when they are likely to be most useful and effective. They are specified in Table 2.3.

These goals are intended to enrich, rather than replace, your instructional goals. For example, in the Beginning Stage when students begin the information problem-solving process and need to identify their research topic, it is important to find ways to help them develop confidence in

Table 2.3. The Motivation Overlay for Information Literacy Skills Instruction

At the Beginning of the Process	During the Process	At the End of the Process
Generate interest in the research process.	Maintain students' interest in the research process.	Encourage students' ongoing confidence in their ability to learn/use information skills.
Establish the importance of attaining information skills.	Promote the value of learning information skills.	Promote students' satisfaction in their research accomplishments.
Build students' confidence in their ability to learn/use information skills.	Reinforce students' confidence in their ability to learn/use information skills.	Motivate continuing information exploration.
Source: Small and Arnone, 2000: 24.		

their ability to identify and refine their topic and complete their research task, using appropriate information resources and technologies. For instance, you might brainstorm various topics with the larger group and then let individuals select a topic from the brainstormed list.

During the research process, as students begin their information exploration, they often feel overwhelmed, confused, and frustrated and their interest in the research task may wane. Therefore, one motivational goal for this stage focuses on ways to maintain their interest in the research process, for example, by varying the way the process is presented to them.

As students come to the end of the process and assess their results, they often feel a sense of relief and satisfaction (or dissatisfaction) with the overall results. Therefore, one motivational goal for the Ending Stage focuses on promoting students' sense of satisfaction in their learning accomplishments (or progress, if they fell short of the learning goals), for example through reflection and self-evaluation.

A motivational goal can be added to one of the skills indicators from the *Standards for the 21st-Century Learner* using the topic of rainforests as the curricular connection.

Adding a Motivational Goal to Instruction

Standard 1.1.5: Evaluate information found in selected sources on the basis of accuracy, validity, appropriateness for needs, importance, and social and cultural context.

Benchmark: When given a list of science websites, students will be able to determine the accuracy, relevance, and comprehensiveness for each site's use in their rainforest research project.

Motivational Goal: Promote the value of learning information skills.

The previous example illustrates how motivational goals enhance the twenty-first-century learning goals by providing an overall relevance to the learning in context. Of course there are many ways to make learning twenty-first-century skills relevant. Another example of a relevance strategy is to teach students how to use a variety of information resources that they will encounter throughout their lives (Breivik and Senn, 1994) and to describe how they might be using these resources in the future. You might even have students provide examples of how they see the adults in their lives using these resources (e.g., reading a print or electronic newspaper to find out what is happening in their community, using a print or online atlas to choose a vacation site, searching a database for the name of an expert). In these examples, the relevance is less tied to the specific classroom-based assignment or resource and more related to acquiring generic life skills.

How Motivation Is Integrated into the *Standards for the 21st-Century Learner*

The AASL Standards embrace motivation as a critical component of inquiry-based learning through the Dispositions in Action strand. Look closely at a number of the indicators and you will see both a motivational component and a possible method of assessment. As examples, let's look at the first two dispositions in action that relate to Standard 1: Inquire, think critically, and gain knowledge.

Standard 1.2.1: Display initiative and engagement by posing questions and investigating the answers beyond the collection of superficial facts.

Displaying initiative and engagement are examples of motivated behaviors. Embedded in this indicator is a way of measuring whether initiative and engagement has occurred. Two possible assessments, then, would be (a) the student asks more questions and (b) the student investigates answers beyond the required learning. In our own research, we have seen the latter in the form of students approaching the librarian and asking for additional resources on a topic after the unit has concluded.

Standard 1.2.2: Demonstrate confidence and self-direction by making independent choices in the selection of resources and formats.

In our motivation overlay, we mentioned that building student confidence in their abilities is an important motivational goal at the beginning stage of research and that maintaining and reinforcing confidence becomes important in later stages. Standard 1.2.2 illustrates that this aspect of motivation is also vital to addressing the Standards. There are many ways of assessing motivation worth discussing.

Motivation Assessment

Earlier, we discussed assessment of instructional goals. You can also assess your motivational goals. One or more motivation measures may be used to determine if each motivational goal has been achieved. Motivational goals are a bit more difficult to assess than instructional goals because they often require more qualitative means for measurement. These are often fuzzier, less precise than the kinds of measures for assessing student learning. Measures of motivation outcomes may range from self-reports to observation of facial clues, from increased question asking to seeking out enrichment opportunities. For example, simple observation might be an appropriate method if your motivational goal is to generate interest in the research process. But what in your observations will tell you this? Perhaps students ask more or better questions about the topic or they appear anxious to get started and excited about beginning their research projects, as reflected in their facial expressions and body language. One exhibition of positive body language is smiling, for example.

> **WORDS OF WISDOM**
>
> The goals you create at the beginning of the lesson planning process are likely to be influenced by the audience analysis you conduct (see Chapter 3). So, keep that eraser at the end of your pencil handy and be ready to revise your goals, if necessary, once you have thoroughly analyzed your learning audience.

Barriers to Success

The educational environment in which you plan to teach your lesson can sometimes present a number of seemingly impenetrable barriers to the success of your lesson. Often, when beginning the lesson planning process, we think about what might prohibit us from achieving our goals and objectives. We start asking those "What if . . . ?" questions, often letting them inhibit the lesson planning process without considering ways to turn them around. For example: What if the sixth grade teaching team doesn't see any value in collaborating with me on this lesson? What if I can't find enough print resources on the Underground Railroad? What if the technology fails during a lesson on how to use the library's databases? What if the biology teachers won't provide enough time for me to accomplish my instructional goals with the students? What if the structure of the daily classroom program makes it almost impossible for me to work with that small group of second graders on particular skills?

There are so many factors that can affect teaching effectiveness and how well students learn. Among other things, these include group size (e.g., too big, too many reading levels), scheduling (e.g., too rigid, too loose, too unpredictable), time (e.g., too little, difficult time of day), the physical facility (e.g., too big, too small, poorly designed), and access to resources/technology (e.g., not enough, unstable, too difficult). All of these present problems requiring flexibility and creative problem solving.

Group Size

The size of the learning audience—how many students are being instructed—can greatly affect instructional planning. In a meta-analysis of 77 studies on class size, Glass and Smith (1978) found that as class size increases, achievement decreases. The greatest gains were when learning groups, particularly with young children, were limited to 15 people or less. Smaller groups allow more individual attention, a broader and deeper curriculum, greater participation, higher achievement, and fewer disciplinary problems. Smaller groups also provide instructors with more time to offer additional instruction and instructional materials (including enrichment) and to monitor the progress of children of varying ability levels. Working with small groups, rather than whole classes, also affects scheduling.

Scheduling

Scheduling is another important environmental factor. Flexible scheduling allows planning for blocks of time so that integrated, resource-based, just-in-time learning can occur; i.e., just when it is needed. If you work in a school with block scheduling, in which larger blocks of time replace smaller class periods, you'll likely find it conducive to building strong collaborative relationships with classroom teachers and to creating constructivist, inquiry-based learning environments in which students have sufficient time to think, question, experiment, practice, work, reflect, and develop understanding and construct knowledge.

A totally fixed schedule in the library often results in just-in-case learning; i.e., students learning something in advance just in case they might need it sometime in the future. This single-period, traditional type of scheduling often leads to a decrease in student interest and perceptions of relevance, an increase in the need for more formal instructional methods, and greater disciplinary problems.

Time

Time can also affect teaching and learning success. Students need enough time to master the required content or skill and construct their knowledge; some need more time than others. You also need enough time to deliver your lesson in a way that allows interaction and participation by students.

Some schools districts have recognized that time limitations are often detrimental to good education. Adopting block scheduling allows schools to break from the traditional fixed-time class periods in order to implement a schedule that is flexible enough to allow extended sessions for instruction that would benefit from more time (Small, 2002). While there has been little research done on the benefits of block scheduling for library programs to date, anecdotal evidence indicates that this may be a promising solution to the problem of lack of sufficient time for teaching and learning information literacy skills.

Physical Facility

The appropriateness of the physical facility is another important environmental factor. One of the authors once worked in a beautiful, large, open library media center in the middle of a brand new school. The facility was warm and inviting and the children loved being there. However, there was only one electrical outlet in the main teaching area. Needless to say, this greatly curtailed her ability to teach using media or technology, except in that one location. Insufficient numbers and placement of electrical outlets, location of windows and radiators, and other physical elements can limit the flexibility and variety of learning activities.

Resources

STOP! THINK! DO!

Using one sheet of paper for each of your goals, fold it in half, making a clear crease down the center. At the top, write the goal. On the left half of the paper, make a list of all of the possible obstacles (what ifs?) to the success of your lesson, leaving space beneath each obstacle. On the right half of the paper, write down all of the enablers that will ensure your lesson's success (e.g., one or more very enthusiastic teacher-collaborators, a supportive technology coordinator, a strong interlibrary loan system), again leaving space below each enabler.

Now, brainstorm one or more strategies for minimizing the weight (strength) of the obstacles and maximizing the weight (strength) of the enablers and write them below each obstacle and enabler. Go back over your brainstormed list and circle the most likely strategies to tip the scales in your favor for each of your lesson's goals. Implement your strategies for lesson success! We sometimes call this activity *Tipping the Scales*. (See Appendix 3 for your "Tipping the Scales" worksheet.)

The availability of sufficient resources also can significantly affect the teacher's ability to teach and the learner's ability to learn. Not enough computers for every student and lack of access to needed materials are just two of the many typical resource problems that can affect the success of a lesson.

If you find yourself playing the "What if . . . ?" game with Resources or any of the other barriers described here, try the Stop! Think! Do! exercise (see sidebar). The exercise is based on Kurt Lewin's (1951) force-field analysis, a problem-solving technique that helps you look at the big picture by analyzing all of the forces impacting the change, weighing the pros and cons, and developing strategies to reduce the impact of the opposing forces and strengthen the supporting forces.

This chapter concludes with an installment of the case study. Don't forget that you can find out more about the adventures of Sally and Harry on the companion website (http://teaching forinquiry.net) for this book!

Case Study #2: Sally and Harry Make Progress

The next day when Harry and Sally officially began their collaboration, Harry initiated the meeting by showing Sally some work he had prepared the night before. He decided it would be better to show her his ideas in writing right away to demonstrate that he was serious about working collaboratively and finding new ways to work together to motivate her students for their research assignment.

Harry showed Sally some possible twenty-first-century learner standards, indicators, and learning benchmarks that he could address that would (1) complement her content standards, (2) support her essential questions for her lesson, and (3) allow him to assess how well students had learned what he would be teaching them. Here is an example of what Harry showed Sally:

- *Standard:* Inquire, think critically, and gain knowledge.

- *Indicator:* Find, evaluate, and select appropriate sources to answer questions.

- *Learning Benchmark:* Understanding the special value of different resource formats, fifth grade students will use at least five appropriate resources, including at least one print, one electronic, and one human resource, to locate information on their topic.

Extension Questions

1. After seeing Harry's first standard, etc., what are one or two others he might include to comprise his lessons that support Sally's unit on Historic Americans?

2. Can you think of one or two activities for Harry's lesson that will help students achieve his learning benchmark?

References

American Association of School Librarians (AASL). 2007. *Standards for the 21st-Century Learner.* Chicago: American Library Association.

American Association of School Librarians (AASL). 2009. *Standards for the 21st-Century Learner in Action.* Chicago: American Library Association.

Anderson, Lorin W., and David R. Krathwohl. 2001. *A Taxonomy for Learning, Teaching, and Assessing: A Revision of Bloom's Taxonomy of Educational Objectives.* New York: Longman.

Arnone, Marilyn P., Ruth V. Small, and Rebecca Reynolds. 2010. "Supporting Inquiry by Identifying Gaps in Student Confidence: Development of a Measure of Perceived Competence." *School Libraries Worldwide* 16, no. 1: 47–60.

Arnone, Marilyn P., Ruth V. Small, and Barbara K. Stripling (Eds.). 2010. *From the Creative Minds of 21st Century Librarians.* Syracuse, NY: Syracuse University Center for Digital Literacy. http://digitalliteracy .syr.edu/data/From_The_Creative_Minds_Book.pdf.

Bloom, Benjamin S. 1956. *Taxonomy of Educational Objectives: The Classification of Educational Goals. Handbook 1: Cognitive Domain.* New York: David McKay.

Bush, Gail. 2003. *The School Buddy System: The Practice of Collaboration.* Chicago: American Library Association.

Breivik, Patricia S., and J. A. Senn. 1994. *Information Literacy: Educating Children for the 21st Century.* New York: Scholastic.

Glass, Gene V., and Mary L. Smith. 1978. *Meta-Analysis of Research on the Relationship of Class-Size and Achievement. The Class Size and Instruction Project.* San Francisco: Far West Lab for Educational Research and Development. ERIC Clearinghouse ED168129.

Gross, June, and Susan Kientz. 1999. "Collaborating for Authentic Learning." *Teacher Librarian* 27, no.1 (October): 21–25.

Harrow, Anita J., 1972. *A Taxonomy of the Psychomotor Domain.* New York: David McKay Co.

Holmes Group. 1990. *Tomorrow's Teachers: A Report of the Holmes Group.* East Lansing, MI: The Holmes Group.

Keller, John M. 1987. "Development and Use of the ARCS Model of Motivational Design." *Journal of Instructional Development* 10, no. 3 (October): 2–10.

Krathwohl, David R., Benjamin Bloom, and Bertram B. Masia. 1964. *Taxonomy of Educational Objectives: Handbook 2: Affective Domain*. Boston: Allyn & Bacon.

Kuhlthau, Carol C. 1989. "Information Search Process: A Summary of Research and Implications for School Library Media Programs." *School Library Media Quarterly* 18 (Fall): 19–25.

———. 1993. "Implementing a Process Approach to Information Skills: A Study Identifying Indicators of Success in Library Media Programs." *School Library Media Quarterly* 22, no.1 (Fall): 11–18.

Lance, Keith C. 2002. "What Research Tells Us About the Importance of School Libraries." *Knowledge Quest* 31, no. 1 (September-October): 17–22.

Lewin, Kurt. 1951. *Field Theory in Social Science: Selected Theoretical Papers*. New York: Harper.

Pitts, Judy M. 1995. "Mental Models of Information: The 1993–94 AASL/Highsmith Research Award Study." *School Library Media Quarterly* 23, no. 3 (Spring): 177–184.

Small, Ruth V. 1999. "An Exploration of Motivational Strategies Used by Library Media Specialists During Library and Information Skills Instruction." *School Library Media Research* 2 (January): 1–22.

———. 2002. "Block Scheduling." Best of ERIC. http://www.ala.org/ala/mgrps/divs/aasl/aaslpubsand journals/slmrb/editorschoiceb/bestoferic/besteric.cfm#block.

———. 2005. *Designing Digital Literacy Programs with IM-PACT: Information Motivation, Purpose, Audience, Content, and Technique*. New York: Neal-Schuman.

Small, Ruth V., and Marilyn P. Arnone. 2000. *Turning Kids on to Research: The Power of Motivation*. Englewood, CO: Libraries Unlimited.

Stipek, Deborah, and Kathy Seal. 2002. "Motivating Minds: Nurturing Your Child's Desire to Learn." *Our Children* 27, no. 5 (March): 7–8.

Stripling, Barbara K., and Judy Pitts. 1988. *Brainstorms and Blueprints: Teaching Library Research as a Thinking Process*. Englewood, CO: Libraries Unlimited.

Todd, Ross J. 1995. "Concept Mapping in Information Science." *Education for Information* 13, no. 4 (December): 333–347.

———. 2003. *School Libraries and Evidence-Based Practice: Dynamics, Strategies and Outcomes*. Presentation to WA School Library Conference. PowerPoint, Slide #5. http://comminfo.rutgers.edu/~rtodd/WA%20Workshop%20Evidence-Based%20Practice.ppt.

Wiggins, Gene, and Jay McTighe. 2005. *Understanding by Design*. Upper Saddle River, NJ: Pearson Education.

DIGGING DEEPER

Arnone, Marilyn P., and Rebecca Reynolds. 2009. "Empirical Support for the Integration of 'Dispositions in Action' and Multiple Literacies into AASL's *Standards for the 21st-Century Learner.*" *School Library Media Research*, 12. American Association of School Librarians. http://www.ala.org/ala/mgrps/divs/aasl/aaslpubsandjournals/slmrb/slmrcontents/volume12/arnone_reynolds.cfm.

Bishop, Kay, and Nancy Larimer. 1999. "Literacy Through Collaboration." *Teacher Librarian* 27, no. 1, 15–20.

Russell, Shayne, 2000. *Teachers and Librarians: Collaborative Relationships*. ERIC Digest, ERIC Clearinghouse on Information and Technology, Syracuse, NY. ED444605.

Simpson, Elizabeth Jane, 1972. "The Classification of Educational Objectives in the Psychomotor Domain." *The Psychomotor Domain* 3: 43–56.

Small, Ruth V. 2006. "Building Collaboration Through Technology." *Journal of Informatics Education Research* 6, no. 2: 61–68.

Utah State Library. 2010. *Outcome-Based Evaluation (OBE): An Overview*. http://library.utah.gov/grants/lsta/evaluation.html.

Students as Learning Audience

The ninth grade U.S. history teacher had instructed a group of 15 students to go to the school library during fifth period (the period right after lunch) to attend a session about databases, something they would need to know for an upcoming research assignment, taught by the high school librarian, Brian Washington. As Mr. Washington proceeded through his PowerPoint lecture followed by a demonstration of the various components of a database, four of the students began texting, three started doodling in their notebooks, and one had fallen asleep. The rest were trying hard to follow Mr. Washington's presentation but didn't understand what a "relational database" is or what "metadata" means and they weren't even sure why they had to learn this stuff anyway. Mr. Washington stopped the lesson momentarily to chastise those students who he thought were not paying attention and then picked up his presentation where he had left off.

Introduction

In this chapter, we refer to learners as your "audience." A learning audience is in some ways similar to and in some ways very different from the audience found at an event such as a play or a hockey game.

For both situations, you work hard to engage your audience and stimulate their interest and excitement about what is happening. But a learning audience is an integral part of the success of the instructional presentation, in ways that the audience at a play or hockey game rarely is. If a few fans or audience members walk away dissatisfied by the experience, it does not substantially affect the success of the event. However, if even one student walks away from your lesson without having been engaged, without learning what was expected of him, or feeling less motivated than when she started, that lesson can be considered a *failure*.

Essential Questions

- What should you know about your learning audience before the instruction begins that will help ensure the success of your inquiry-based instruction?
- How does knowing as much as possible about your learners help you design more effective inquiry-based instruction?

Chapter Outcomes and Indicators

After the completion of Chapter 3 and taking advantage of other learning opportunities in this book's companion website (http://teachingforinquiry.net), you should achieve these learning outcomes and indicators:

1. OUTCOME: Know how to create a "profile" of your learning audience.
   a. INDICATOR: Describe characteristics of your learning audience.
   b. INDICATOR: Determine the AASL Standards and Indicators that most appropriately match your learning audience's profile.
2. OUTCOME: Understand the factors in your learning environment that could positively or negatively influence the success of your lesson.
   a. INDICATOR: Design strategies that maximize those environmental factors that support learning success.
   b. INDICATOR: Design strategies that minimize or eliminate those environmental factors that represent obstacles to learning success.

Analyzing Your Learning Audience

As your instructional planning journey continues, you will need to learn something about those learners who are traveling with you. As school librarians, our traveling partners are a diverse bunch, with different backgrounds, experiences, and interests. While you cannot predict with 100 percent certainty what each learner needs in order to learn successfully, conducting a learning audience analysis, added to what you understand from Chapter 2 about your lesson's purpose, will move you closer toward designing effective lessons for all learners.

> ### STOP! THINK! DO!
>
> Do you remember what it was like when you were a student? Perhaps you are a student now or perhaps you haven't been a student in many years. Either way, I bet you can remember, even picture, a memorable instructor. What was it about him or her that made learning an exciting and meaningful experience for you? What did *you* bring to the experience that increased its potential to be exciting and meaningful?

Knowing as much information about your learning audience as possible will help you make appropriate decisions about what to teach, how much to teach (and how much students should explore independently), and how to teach it. This requires you to act as a kind of *information detective*, collecting a wide variety of information about your learners to determine some of the (1) general characteristics they bring as a group (e.g., class, reading group, library club); (2) individual differences that exist within a group (e.g., learning styles, life experiences, interests); and (3) history of their collective and individual learning experiences and accomplishments. The more specific information you are able to gather about the groups and individual members of your learning audience *before* you plan your instruction, the better.

While we often view groups as monolithic (e.g., a third grade class, the drama club), they are typically far from that. The individual characteristics of students within a group or class contribute to the diversity, complexity, and dynamics of the group or class as a whole. This requires differentiated instruction and alternatives for learning that address individual differences.

Individual Differences

Today's learners are diverse in many ways, including such considerations as culture, ethnicity, abilities, and languages, as well as differences in learning interests, motivations, and preferred learning methods. For example, sometimes *different* learners prefer the same content in different forms (e.g., visual, audio, text) and sometimes the *same* learner prefers to learn different content in different presentation formats (e.g., discussions, games, slides with voiceover narration).

Many individual difference factors can affect how much and how well students learn from instructional and learning activities, as well as learner perceptions of the content presented. Individual differences range from personal characteristics (e.g., age, gender, physical limitations) to educational background (e.g., grade level, reading level) and from group characteristics (e.g., number of students, grouping) to incoming motivation (e.g., personal goals, interests). These differences can influence both an individual's *desire* to learn and his *ability* to learn.

Teaching a group will likely include a variety and range of characteristics to consider. Group dynamics and interactions among all members of the group affect learning within the group. For example, learning is more effective in groups in which a sense of community has been created where learners feel significant and respected (Tomlinson, 2000).

The more you know about your target population, your learning audience, the better you can prepare an instructional environment that effectively meets their needs. The information you discover about your learning audience will affect the amount and type of content you cover, the instructional techniques you choose, and learning outcomes.

There are several questions you might want to answer as part of your learning audience analysis that will allow tailoring instruction to the backgrounds and learning needs of students. Here are some of them:

- What are their ages and developmental levels?
- What are their educational and reading levels?
- How large is the group?
- Why are they there (voluntary vs. required)?
- What do they already know about this topic?
- Are there students with special learning needs?
- Is English a second language for some students?

Sometimes we assume some of this information. For example, we may assume that a group of sixth graders will be of a certain age and developmental level and will have reached a particular learning level. However, we soon learn that there may be a range of ages, abilities, and maturity levels in a single group and that, while some may have mastered particular knowledge and skills, others may not have.

Noted child development researcher Jean Piaget (1929) found that certain patterns of intellectual development corresponded with a child's age. These patterns can be helpful when planning instruction for groups of a certain age range or grade level.

According to the Child Development Institute (2011), children ages four to six are still at a preoperational phase in which concepts are crudely formed and seen only from their own perspective (egocentricism), they easily believe in fantasy, and they are not yet able to form their own rules of behavior. For example, in relation to the New York City Inquiry Benchmark Skills (see Chapter 4), these children should be able to follow a modeled inquiry process, ask "I wonder" questions about a given topic, and begin to distinguish fact from fiction.

Children at the concrete operations phase (ages 7–11) begin to think and reason logically and in an organized fashion. They can perform multiple categorization tasks and solve concrete problems but are not yet able to handle abstract reasoning. As children move into the formal operations phase (ages 12 to adulthood), they are able to think and reason more abstractly, generate and test hypotheses, and predict outcomes. Even with the explosion of information and learning technologies, Piaget's (1929) phases of development are as relevant today as ever for consideration in lesson planning. According to the NYC Inquiry Benchmark Skills, these children should be able, for example, to ask questions to clarify topics, search an online catalog, and form opinions.

Researcher Jerome Bruner (1986, 1996) was also interested in the cognitive levels on which children operated. He maintained that any child, no matter what age or grade level, can learn anything as long as it is presented on that child's cognitive level. In our context, this means that skills specified by the *Standards for the 21st-Century Learner* can be taught even to kindergarteners, as long as they are presented in simple, concrete, and familiar terms. This is important to know when teaching such abstract concepts and processes to very young children. Following the NYC Inquiry Benchmark Skills matrix (Table 4.1 in Chapter 4, p. 72) horizontally, we can see that students in grades K–2 should be able to ask "I wonder" questions but as they move into grades 3–5, they are now able to assess those questions and predict answers, while in grades 6–8 they should be able to refine their questions and, once in high school, plan their own systematic inquiry project.

The more specific information you are able to gather about the individual members of your learning audience *before* you develop your instruction, the better. Having this type of information can help ensure lesson success; lacking some or all of it can lead to lesson failure. This information can also help you plan ways to provide additional or more specific instructional scaffolding where needed.

While much of the important learner information cited earlier, such as age, reading level, and gender, can be discovered through your collaborative planning sessions with classroom teachers, there is a great deal of important information that will not be as clearly defined using this method. Here are a few other learner characteristics that you might want to consider when planning and delivering your twenty-first-century skills instruction.

Cognitive Styles

Cognitive style denotes the way one processes information. For example, one person might read an article and come away with some general, overall view of the content of that article, while another person reading the same article may remember specific facts in the article. One focuses more on the broad overview; the other focuses more on the details. A learner's cognitive style can influence, among other things, the amount of structure he needs in his educational environment and the type of reinforcement used to enhance learning (Summerville, 1998).

Probably the most frequently cited work on cognitive styles is that of Herman Witkin and associates (1977), who found that people's preferred way of perceiving, thinking about, and solving information problems stretched along a continuum. On one end, people tend to be *synthesizers* or *field dependent*; that is, more intuitive, global thinkers, who often prefer to understand *the big picture* and are influenced by the surrounding field (context). In learning situations, field dependent learners prefer a more holistic presentation of the content to be learned, such as an agenda or overview, before moving on to learning its various components. For instance, showing your students one or two examples of a completed research project like the one they have been assigned, will allow those who are more global thinkers to understand the whole and then begin to concentrate on each of the pieces needed to successfully complete the assignment.

On the other end of Witkin et al.'s (1977) continuum are those who tend to be *analyzers* or *field independent*, in which the learner analyzes the information, discriminating elements from the field (context), preferring to think about or manipulate the various parts of a problem before assembling them into the larger whole. These types of learners might like to see all of the component parts of a project first and then, at the end, understand how they may be synthesized.

These analyzers often prefer learning situations that they can structure for themselves; they thrive in an inquiry-based learning environment. They seek opportunities to have more control over their own learning experiences (Garger and Guild, 1984). Therefore, creating learning environments in which analyzers can assume more responsibility and independence during the learning experience will be highly motivating to them.

It is important to remember that cognitive styles fall along a continuum and that few people are at one extreme end or the other. Generally, most of us tend to be more one than the other but might shift preferences, depending on the situation. Therefore, we recommend giving all students at least *some* autonomy over their learning, providing choices that allow them to learn what is interesting to them and opportunities for independence in pursuing their learning as far as they can.

Learning Styles

Learning styles differ from cognitive styles in their focus. Cognitive styles indicate how a person prefers to receive and process information, while learning styles indicate ways in which a person appears to prefer to learn and the ways he or she seems to learn best. For example, some learners prefer to learn through text, some through visuals, others through audio means, and still others through multiple media. Some learners prefer manipulating physical objects while others may prefer manipulating objects on a computer screen; some may prefer verbal information presented orally by a teacher, while others prefer it textually via an e-reader.

David Kolb's (1984) work on experiential learning identified four stages to the learning cycle: concrete experience, observation and reflection, abstract concept formation, and new applications, understanding that a learner might enter a learning episode at any of these stages. Although Kolb thought of these stages as a cycle that one moves through over time, he found that, in general, people tend to have one of four preferred learning styles. Based on this knowledge, Kolb developed an instrument, the *Learning Style Inventory*, to assess a learner's dominant learning style.

Kolb (1984) classified learning styles into four categories: *Divergers* prefer to have information presented to them in a detailed, systematic, reasoned manner, while *Assimilators* prefer getting their information from an expert, presented in an accurate and organized fashion. *Convergers* are motivated by activities that allow them to discover how things work and understand why they work the way they do, while *Accommodators* prefer to be more active participants in their learning.

A number of instruments are available for measuring learning styles, but students' learning styles, like their cognitive styles, can vary depending on the purpose and content of what they are learning, thus affecting the way in which it is presented and learned. For example, while my preferred learning style for learning the history of opera might be reading a book about it, my preference might change to audio or audiovisual methods for learning about a specific opera. Understanding the importance of learning and cognitive styles for teaching for inquiry rests in the awareness that such styles demand differentiated instructional methods and learning activities, resources, and technologies.

> ## CHECKPOINT
>
> The first part of this chapter has focused on a range of learner characteristics to consider when planning your lessons, from individual learner traits like age, gender, and reading level to group factors such as grade level, group size, and homogeneous versus heterogeneous to environmental concerns such as size of learning space, arrangement of furniture, and number of electrical outlets. We've also described how cognitive style and learning style can influence the way a learner approaches a learning task.

Now, we move into another, and perhaps the most vital, characteristic, the motivation to learn. Building on the motivation goals stated in the motivation overlay presented in Chapter 2, we describe a motivation model that offers you a powerful tool for ensuring your learning environment maximizes student motivation.

Learner Motivation

We all would love to have a class filled with intrinsically motivated students who thrive on inquiry and exploration and have a passion for learning. However, while we may have a few students with those characteristics or may have a majority of students with those characteristics some of the time, we quickly realize that most of our students are often disinterested in twenty-first-century learning skills unless they have a specific question or problem (assigned or personal) for which they will need those skills. Therefore, these skills *must* be taught at the moment of need.

When young children begin the schooling process, most are highly curious and can be or already are easily motivated to learn. But as the years go on and as a result of an accumulation of both positive and negative learning experiences, students have formed attitudes toward learning in general and specifically toward you as the instructor, the kind of instruction you are providing, and the learning environment you have created. In addition, as students grow and develop, they face an ever-growing plethora of distractions in the world (e.g., peer groups, texting, videos) that increasingly influence how, when, and what they learn.

Raymond Wlodkowski (1993) found that learners come to the learning experience with preestablished needs and attitudes that potentially affect their learning outcomes. This is consistent with constructivist philosophy, which states that for effective learning to occur, instruction must address the experiences and contexts that make the student willing and able to become engaged in the learning process.

Needs and Attitudes

Perhaps the best-known researcher on human needs is Abraham Maslow. Maslow (1943) identified five categories of needs that all humans possess. These needs are hierarchical in nature; each preceding level must be considered before moving up to the next higher level need. The five categories of needs range from basic physiological and safety needs to acceptance and self-esteem, and finally, to realizing one's potential to the fullest degree (what Maslow calls "self-actualization").

Maslow's Hierarchy of Needs is as relevant today as it was when it was first introduced. For example, it may provide more of a challenge for you to engage students in learning if they come to you with their lower-level needs unmet. If they are feeling hungry, tired, or unsafe, no matter how great your lesson is, it is unlikely that your learning goals will be met.

Safety and security, both physical and psychological, are an essential part of any constructivist learning environment. Unfortunately, in today's world students often feel physically unsafe in our schools. At all levels and in every type of community, there are increasing signs of this—from alarm systems to surveillance cameras to armed police patrolling school hallways. This vulnerability affects teachers and students alike.

In addition to physical security, psychological security issues abound. As you move up the hierarchy to needs for acceptance and self-esteem, you can easily understand the importance of providing a supportive learning environment in which students feel safe to make mistakes and try out new ideas while expressing opinions without punishment or penalty.

Unfortunately, we can all find examples of nonsupportive learning environments from kindergarten through graduate school. Here's such an example, taken from data in a study by Small, Dodge, and Jiang (1996), who were investigating the factors that make instruction interesting or boring to students. It is unlikely that the students in this college class felt psychologically safe in this learning environment.

> *The class was supposed to be a Friday morning seminar class in elementary education in which students would participate in a discussion of problems and issues directly related to student teaching. . . . Roll was called precisely at 8 a.m., with tardy marks given to those not present (all students were in fifth-year college work). The content of the class was a step-by-step demonstration of how to make a pocket chart. Students were required to follow each step and perform the task. Negative remarks were directed at individual students by the instructor if they did not have the right materials or if they did not follow the exact directions. I was told to do one procedure over because I had taken a shortcut.*

Building a supportive learning environment is especially important for adolescents for whom the need to belong, preserve their self-esteem, and attain peer approval is especially strong. Supporting learners' confidence and feelings of self-esteem can be accomplished by (1) helping them gain mastery, i.e., to acquire the skills and knowledge they need to become competent, and (2) creating opportunities to gain attention and recognition for their achievements.

Students also come to a learning situation with preformed attitudes, shaped largely by past experiences. While we all come into existence full of curiosity for exploring our world, in inquiry-based learning environments, curiosity is a critical component for determining the type and amount of a learner's exploration and engagement and for promoting an intrinsic motivation to learn (Small and Arnone, 1998/1999). You may be aware of the unfortunate phenomenon, first identified by researcher Susan Harter (e.g., 1981), of an increasing decline in children's curiosity from about third grade until about eighth grade, never really returning to its original high level. This phenomenon provides even more justification for designing inquiry-based instruction.

> **STOP! THINK! DO!**
>
> To what can we attribute this decline in curiosity? Do you think it is a natural phenomenon or is it influenced by the child's environment? What role might schooling play in this decline? How might the learning environment you create help to counteract this decline?

You may also have encountered learners who don't even seem to want to try to learn something new. Not only does it seem as if the curiosity has been drained out of them, but they honestly believe they cannot learn, no matter how hard they try. Often they place the blame for this on external factors (perhaps even you).

A student who has experienced repeated failure, does not perceive his actions as having any influence on his subsequent success or failure, and consistently attributes negative outcomes to external forces may have developed a condition known as "learned helplessness" (Seligman, 1975). Students who are learned helpless lack confidence in their ability to learn, believe they have no control over their own learning, and feel that, no matter what they do, they will fail. Learning no longer has value for them and they have only an expectation for failure, often seeking ways to avoid learning situations entirely (e.g., cutting classes, skipping school). In school, they typically give up before they even start, making no effort at all, even in situations where clearly they are able to succeed. You will often observe students who are learned helpless exhibiting either withdrawal or acting-out behaviors during instruction.

The good news is that there are motivational teaching strategies that can be employed to help eliminate these behaviors and, used consistently and over time, can reverse these feelings of learned helplessness and the decline in curiosity. For example, information technologies are a powerful tool for providing each learner with autonomy for individualizing his or her learning experience. Technology allows the learned helpless student to set her own pace and have choices in how much, when, and what she will learn in a supportive learning environment as she begins to experience some learning success. Technology also can be used to ignite a learner's curiosity and the freedom to pursue that curiosity as much or as little as he wishes, individually or with others, via social networks for example. Such technologies "can play a role in triggering and addressing personal, situational, and contextual factors that support autonomy and competence and engender active, deep learning" (Arnone et al., 2011: 182).

Motivational Profile

Understanding these incoming needs and attitudes will help you, as an instructor, to design a learning environment that is more closely aligned to students' needs and fosters positive attitudes toward learning. One way to do that is to create a motivational profile of your learning audience, using Keller's (1987) ARCS Model, that provides a framework for designing an inquiry-based learning environment that meets the motivational (as well as the learning) needs of students. For example, you might want to know the following about your learning audience:

- Are students curious about information exploration and excited about learning *or* do they find it just plain *boring*? (Attention)

- Are students interested in learning inquiry skills and see them as valuable *or* do they perceive these skills as disconnected from their lives? (Relevance)

- Do students believe they have the prerequisite information skills and knowledge needed to successfully achieve the stated learning objectives *or* do they lack feelings of confidence and self-determination because of past failures? (Confidence)

- Do students take responsibility for their learning successes or failures *or* do they lay credit or blame on others? (Satisfaction)

Answers to questions such as these will help you design appropriate instructional interventions to meet the motivational needs of your students. Let's examine each of these questions in a bit more depth.

> *Are students curious about information exploration and excited about learning or do they find it just plain boring?*

Students may have had some past positive experiences with motivating lessons on inquiry learning, making their attention or interest level high or these lessons could have been presented in a boring manner, thereby causing them to have a low level of incoming interest.

Keller (1979: 31) defined curiosity as a motive to reduce a person's "responsiveness to incongruity and uncertainty" and cites it as the primary theoretical basis for the Attention component of the ARCS Model. Day defined curiosity as "a state of excitement and directed interest" (Day, 1982: 19). He described it in terms of (1) a need for exploration of one's environment to reduce uncertainty and (2) as a search for information leading to knowledge (Small and Arnone, 1998/1999). We are all born curious, a notion easily supported just by watching a baby explore his environment.

There is, however, another type of curiosity, first identified by noted researcher Daniel Berlyne (1960) who called this type of curiosity *epistemic curiosity,* i.e., curiosity that can only be resolved through the closing of an information gap and the acquisition of knowledge. It is this type of intellectual curiosity that you, as an instructor, should try to stimulate by, for example, posing perplexing problems or thought-provoking questions or letting students bring their own problems and questions to the learning situation. This can arouse students' epistemic curiosity and desire for information exploration (Small and Arnone, 2000).

Small, Dodge, and Jiang (1996) found that students consider interesting instruction that is colorful, effective, and personal. They also discovered that when learners feel competent, and are presented with complex and difficult (challenging) content, interest in learning increases.

> *Are students interested in learning inquiry skills and see them as valuable or do they perceive these skills as disconnected from their lives?*

If students have learned inquiry skills when they needed them (that "just-in-time" learning mentioned earlier), linked to class activities or assignments, they are likely to approach your instruction believing what they learn will have relevance to their lives. If those skills were taught out of context or at a time other than when they are needed ("just-in-case" learning), their relevance would be perceived as questionable. In our scenario at the beginning of the chapter, the librarian was teaching students about databases for a research project that hadn't yet been assigned, thereby rendering their perceptions of the instruction as irrelevant, as demonstrated by their behaviors (e.g., texting, sleeping).

As you design your instruction, your students' personal needs and interests can be addressed by tying inquiry learning directly to the curriculum and students' assignments and projects. As you develop your examples, support materials, and media, in addition to addressing student needs and interests, you might consider the diversity of your learning audience so that all students find relevance in your instruction.

> *Do students believe they have the prerequisite information skills and knowledge needed to successfully achieve the stated learning objectives or do they lack feelings of confidence and self-determination because of past failures?*

If students have had prior successful experiences in learning and using inquiry skills, they will have developed feelings of competence. Feelings of competence are also important to what AASL refers to as "dispositions in action." Dispositions include curiosity, creativity, and reading for enjoyment, among others. Arnone and Reynolds (2009) explored curiosity as a disposition driven by the need for competence. Developing feelings of competence in inquiry skills should allow students to remain in a zone of curiosity because they have the skills to continue to explore for information until their curiosity questions are satisfactorily resolved and, indeed, the researchers found a significant correlation between perceived competence in inquiry skills and curiosity. Therefore, not having such skills runs the risk of killing curiosity before it even has a chance to be fully ignited.

Earlier, we described the concept of learned helplessness, when students are likely to doubt their ability to learn and may experience feelings of being out of control and helpless. One effective technique for preventing this learned helplessness when teaching inquiry skills is to find ways to help these vulnerable students gain required knowledge and skills through review, coaching, and reteaching. For students experiencing learning difficulty and with a high need for affiliation, it can often help to pair them with those who have mastered the content, acting as coaches. The research says that *both* the student coach and the student who is coached will experience increased achievement and motivation (Finn, 1987).

Most students begin the formal schooling experience wanting and expecting to be successful learners. In our experience, most students will try to live up to the expectations you set for them, so set *high* (but attainable) expectations. If you explain exactly what students are expected to learn, communicate your high expectations to them, clearly demonstrate how to accomplish the learning task, and provide enough time, guidance, and support along the way, the research confirms that your students will have greater and more frequent learning success (Finn, 1987), come closer to reaching Maslow's highest level of need—self-actualization (or reaching one's potential), and avoid sinking into learned helplessness.

> *Do students take responsibility for their learning successes or failures or do they lay credit or blame on others?*

When students are held accountable for their own learning progress, they have a higher potential for learning satisfaction. Whether students succeed or fail at a learning task, it is important for them to acknowledge their influence on the outcome. In a research study to determine how students rate a number of instructional attribute terms (including the *student* and the *instructor*) in relation to each of the ARCS components, Small and Gluck (1994) found that participants rated both *instructor* and *student* as among the closest terms to all four ARCS components. The authors concluded that, while students perceived the instructor as having a critical role in achieving the four ARCS components, they also perceived themselves as sharing that responsibility. We, as instructors, should encourage this perception.

When students do not take responsibility for their own learning, who do they credit or blame? Motivation theorists such as Bernard Weiner (1972) found that people attribute one of four explanations to their success or failure at a task. Those who internalize the responsibility for their own learning ascribe such learning to their *ability*, which has less to do with IQ and more to do with possessing the prerequisite knowledge and skills to be successful, and their *effort*. After completing a learning task, a person with an internal attribution might comment, "I was successful because I worked hard on my research project" or "I failed because I did not take time to evaluate the quality of the web resources I used for my research project." In both cases, the attribution has been internalized; the person takes responsibility for the learning outcome. Alfie Kohn (1993) believes that this internalization is essential for developing a pattern of life-long learning.

Those who externalize the results of their learning ascribe these outcomes to either the *difficulty of the task* (e.g., "I succeeded because the assignment was so easy" or "I failed because the assignment was too hard") or to *luck* (e.g., "I did well on that research project because I was carrying my lucky coin" or "I did poorly because teachers don't like me"). In all of these cases, the student is attributing success or failure to external forces rather than taking responsibility for his own learning. Brophy (1986) recommends helping students develop a more internal attribution, where the reward is in the learning task itself, by focusing on the task at hand rather than dwelling on past failures, using review and reflection to identify mistakes or alternative ways to approach the learning task, and personal accountability; i.e., attributing their failure to a lack of effort, insufficient information, or use of ineffective learning strategies, rather than external forces.

While we may agree that all of the factors discussed above contribute to an understanding of the learning and motivational needs of students, how can you obtain this information *before* you implement your instruction? Certainly, you can get some of this information from classroom teachers and others who have worked with your target audience in the past. Some factors, like reading levels and age of students, are documented in student records. But how can you find out what students want to learn, what motivates them, what their attitudes are toward the instruction you are planning, and so forth?

One method is to ask the students themselves before the instruction begins. It's amazing how even very young children can express their learning needs and interests. You can ask them orally or you can ask older students to respond in writing to a set of questions that explore both their prior knowledge and incoming motivation, such as:

- What don't you know about your topic that you would like to know?
- What is the most important thing you want to learn about your topic?
- What questions do you have about your topic *right now*?
- What might be fun to know about your topic?
- What can I do to help you be successful on your research project?

> **TAKING ACTION**
>
> Using some of the knowledge and motivation questions or your own questions, design a brief paper-based survey for students in your school that you could have them complete the next time they're in the library. We bet you will learn things about them that you didn't know before that will help you the next time you need to design instruction for them.

By always thinking about your learning audience and how you can make your instruction more inquiry-based and student-centered, you will soon develop a whole toolkit of motivational strategies you can use. Gathering information like the above will allow customization of instruction for your learning audience and maximize the potential for learning satisfaction for all students. For example, if you find out that some third graders are really interested in dinosaurs, you can have them articulate the questions they have about dinosaurs and explore with them ways to find the answers to their questions. Tenth grade biology students required to complete a research study on a specific topic might be more motivated by highlighting bibliography or bookmarking websites that provide the richest resources they might use that will help them be successful.

Creating a motivational profile provides you with additional information for a richer and deeper understanding of your learners and greater insight into how to design teaching strategies to meet their learning and motivational needs. To create a motivational profile, you will want to assess their incoming motivation using high, medium, and low ratings of (1) your learners' interest in your topic (e.g., evaluating web resources) in order to rate their probable *attention* throughout your lesson, (2) the *relevance* of the topic to your learners' needs and interests (e.g., they are using the web resources for their class project), (3) how *confident* your learners will be that they can learn what you want them to learn, and (4) the potential satisfaction your learners will feel if they successfully learn.

Often, a group's motivation varies and your motivational profile will reflect that variation. Here is an example of motivational profiles created by preservice school librarian Jennifer Adams. Jennifer designed a lesson plan for ninth grade students in collaboration with the English teacher in which students would create a Wordle of quotes as part of a presentation on Steinbeck's *Of Mice and Men*. Her motivational profile of the class looked like this:

> **Attention:** Low, Medium, or High—A lot of this depends upon whether or not the students liked reading the book *Of Mice and Men*. If they liked reading it, then they will probably be likely to want to do the project on it. Some of them may be in the middle with regards to liking the story and therefore may be a little involved with doing the project. Lastly, some students may not have liked the book at all so they probably won't be very happy about doing a project on it.
>
> **Relevance:** High—The students just finished reading the book in class and have a lot of knowledge of what it is about. They have to do a presentation on it in which they use a visual aid, created from Wordle, to display a quote or a few quotes that describe a theme or two from the story.
>
> **Confidence:** Medium—They already know what the book is about so this will help them with their project but they don't know how to use Wordle yet. I will be teaching them how to use it. They might be a little nervous about using it for the first time.
>
> **Satisfaction Potential:** High—The students have been told by their teacher what the expectations are for the assignment. They need to complete it using Wordle and the book *Of Mice and Men*. Each of them will create one or a few visual aids with Wordle, which they will eventually show to the class in their presentations. Their work will be displayed for others to see which will hopefully give them a sense of pride in their final products. (Small, 2005: 87–88)

Giving some thought to the motivational profile of any individual or group of learners will enhance the quality of a lesson and its probability for success.

When you teach groups of students, you must assume that a full range of learning styles, cognitive styles, and motivation levels is represented. As an instructor, it is your responsibility to try to match the needs of these varying levels. But how do you do this, especially when you might be facing a class of twenty or more individuals with different learning styles, cognitive styles, reading levels, maturity levels, and personal goals and interests? It is almost overwhelming to think of the wide variety of individual differences among students.

One useful way to think about meeting the multiple needs and styles of each learner is through the Center for Applied Special Technology's (CAST) Universal Design for Learning principles (CAST, 2011). Universal Design for Learning (UDL) suggests using flexible teaching methods (multiple means of representation), demonstrations of student learning (multiple means of action and expression), and motivation techniques (multiple means of engagement) so that any learning episode can be tailored by and for the individual learner's needs, regardless of ability. Application of UDL principles to inquiry-based teaching and learning will result in learning environments that address the range of needs and abilities within a learning audience. For example, if you wish to create a website on inquiry learning skills for students, you will need to consider font size, use of color, closed captioning, video transcriptions, and other issues that would affect the success of some or all of your learners.

Environmental Aspects of Teaching and Learning in the Library

Environmental factors can affect (both positively and negatively) the quality of both inquiry-based teaching and learning. A bright and cheerful learning environment in which learning is seen as an interactive process can go a long way toward motivating both students and the librarian. While a school librarian with excellent teaching skills certainly can enhance the learning experience, it is the learner who has ultimate control over what motivates and engages him to learn and what doesn't. However, the librarian can create a learning environment that is conducive to stimulating that motivation and engagement.

The research on learning environments can help instructors better understand how and when students learn best. For example, research on sound indicates that, while we may find sound distracting to our concentration, adolescents typically have an increased need for sound while learning (Dunn, Beaudry, and Klavas, 1989). (Parents who ask their teenage students to turn off the radio while they are doing their homework might want to rethink that request.) Knowing this, you may wish to consider occasionally having music playing in the background during instruction with high school students.

Other research has found that the need for *less* light appears to be important for young children; conversely, too much light has sometimes been linked to hyperactive behavior. However, the research also shows that older children require *more light* (Dunn, Beaudry, and Klavas, 1989). Therefore, a brightly lit library may be more conducive to learning for middle and high school students.

Perhaps not surprisingly, the research also indicates that boys tend to need to physically move more than girls during a learning session (Dunn, Beaudry, and Klavas, 1989). Building in activities that require movement and adjusting sound and light to the needs of your learning audience will help provide a physical environment conducive to learning and engagement.

In our scenario at the beginning of this chapter, Mr. Washington recognized that he had a problem. First of all, the period after lunch requires "super-motivation" because people often feel more drowsy and lethargic after eating a meal. This means that sedentary learning (e.g., lecture-based) can torpedo any lesson that is presented right after lunch and an instructor may have to pull strategies from his motivation toolbox that require movement and active participation to overcome those sleepy feelings. In this case, Mr. Washington might have anticipated this and scheduled his lesson in a computer lab where students can access databases, input data, search for information, etc. Providing students with a list of action items that need to be physically checked off as they are completed, randomly calling on individual students to provide information at key points in the instruction, having students participate in an active game that illustrates key ideas for learning, or asking

CHECKPOINT

This chapter has focused on the learning audience—your students—and the importance of knowing as much about them as needed in order to design an engaging and interesting learning episode. Conducting a learning audience analysis is intended to uncover as much as you can about your learners' current knowledge, skills, and attitudes in order to make appropriate decisions about what to teach, how much to teach, and how to teach it.

individuals or small groups of students to teach parts of a lesson to the rest of the class are a few ideas that counteract the after-lunch blahs. Creating inquiry-based, constructivist learning environments requires a focus on learner outcomes, rather than lesson content, and on finding ways to motivate and engage students in the learning process.

While all of the factors described in this chapter may be useful when planning instruction, it is unlikely that you would or should include all of them every time you create a lesson or unit plan. However, the recognition and understanding of the broad variety of relevant characteristics of both the group and its individual members and the consideration of the most critical characteristics of your learning audience will allow you to plan more effectively.

WORDS OF WISDOM

While this chapter has described a number of strategies for increasing your students' motivation, your own excitement about learning can be the greatest motivator of all.

TAKING ACTION

Try substituting your own motivational teaching ideas for those presented in Table 3.1 or add some new ones to each box.

Return to Inquiry + Motivation

Table 3.1 integrates inquiry and motivation to get started on ways you might use inquiry motivation as a framework for designing an inquiry-based lesson. You will see the six inquiry phases in column one and an example of a relevant motivational strategy with related ARCS component in column two.

Case Study #3: Harry and Sally Consider Motivation

While Harry and Sally had talked about some of the characteristics of her class, they had not yet talked about the students' incoming motivation. Some of Sally's students still demonstrated a curiosity for learning, while several others seemed to have become disinterested in school. Four students were labeled "gifted" and Sally mentioned she always had a hard time keeping those students "busy." "They are always asking questions," she said, "and I can't answer all of them. It

Table 3.1. Inquiry Phases and Relevant Motivation Strategies with Related ARCS Components

Inquiry Phase	Motivation Strategies (with Related ARCS Components)
Connect	Provide links between inquiry skills and classroom assignments. (Relevance)
Wonder	Invite students to submit questions they would like to explore to a Feedback Box in the library. (Relevance, Confidence)
Investigate	Teach students how to evaluate websites to ensure credibility of their work. (Confidence, Satisfaction)
Construct	Allow students to choose and independently create their learning product using their desired format, providing guidance where needed. (Attention, Relevance, Confidence, Satisfaction)
Express	Allow students to use social media to share knowledge. (Attention, Satisfaction)
Reflect	Help students identify ways they could improve on the type of assignment in the future. (Confidence, Satisfaction)

makes me feel uncomfortable." Sally also mentioned to Harry that two of the boys had learning disabilities and one of them had an IEP (individualized educational program). Both of these students lacked confidence in their learning ability and seemed to only hang out with each other. She mentioned that last year, almost every time these two boys came to the library, the former librarian had to reprimand them or send them back to the classroom.

All in all, Sally's students represented a wide range of motivation levels. Harry and Sally knew they had their work cut out for them with this group of students. Sally thought reverting to the paper assignment might, in the end, save her a lot of time and effort while making changes might not pay off if the students' differences complicated the project too much. She put those thoughts aside, though, thinking instead of the motivation Harry had for helping these students really become interested in the projects and the increased learning potential of this project.

Note: Before you move on to the following Extension Questions, please visit our companion website (http://teachingforinquiry.net) for more details on Harry and Sally's learning audience analysis, including a motivational profile of Sally's class.

Extension Questions

1. Is it possible for Sally and Harry to make effective changes to this project, given the results of the motivational profile? Would it be easier for them to create the project plan after they meet and interact with the students? Should they proceed with their plans?

2. Do Harry and Sally need to consider all of the information that they have about the students when designing the plan? Is any information not relevant to their planning? Should they try to learn any other information before continuing?

References

Arnone, Marilyn P., and Rebecca Reynolds. 2009. "Empirical Support for the Integration of 'Dispositions in Action' and Multiple Literacies into AASL's *Standards for the 21st-Century Learner*." School Library Media Research, 12. American Library Association. http://www.ala.org/ala/mgrps/divs/aasl/aaslpubs andjournals/slmrb/slmrcontents/volume12/arnone_reynolds.cfm.

Arnone, Marilyn P., Ruth V. Small, Sarah Chauncey, and Patricia McKenna. 2011. "Curiosity, Interest and Engagement in Technology-Pervasive Learning Environments: A New Research Agenda." *Educational Technology Research and Development* 59: 181–198.

Berlyne, Daniel E. 1960. *Conflict, Arousal, and Curiosity*. New York: McGraw-Hill.

Brophy, Jere. 1986. *Socializing Student Motivation to Learn*. Research Series No. 169. Washington: Office of Educational Research and Improvement (ED).

Bruner, Jerome S. 1986. "Play, Thought and Language." *Prospects: Quarterly Review of Education* 16, no.1: 77–83.

———.1996. "What We Have Learned about Early Learning." *European Early Childhood Education Research Journal* 4, no.1: 5–16.

Center for Applied Special Technology (CAST). 2011. "CAST: Learning Tools." CAST, Inc. Accessed June 3. http://www.cast.org/learningtools/index.html.

Child Development Institute. 2011. "Stages of Intellectual Development in Children and Teenagers." Child Development Institute. Accessed June 3. http://www.childdevelopmentinfo.com/development/piaget.shtml.

Day, Hi I. 1982. "Curiosity and the Interested Explorer." *Performance and Instruction* 21, no. 4 (May): 19–22.

Dunn, Rita, Jeffrey S. Beaudry, and Angela Klavas. 1989. "Survey of Research on Learning Styles." *Educational Leadership* 46, no. 6 (March): 50–58.

Finn, Chester E. Jr. 1987. *What Works: Research About Teaching and Learning.* Washington, DC: U.S. Department of Education.

Garger, Stephen, and Pat Guild. 1984. "Learning Styles: The Crucial Differences." *Curriculum Review* 23, no. 1 (February): 9–12.

Harter, Susan. 1981. "A New Self-Report Scale of Intrinsic versus Extrinsic Orientation in the Classroom: Motivational and Informational Components." *Developmental Psychology*, 17, no. 3 (May): 300–312.

Keller, John M. 1979. "Motivation and Instructional Design: A Theoretical Perspective." *Journal of Instructional Development* 2, no. 4 (Summer): 26–34.

———. 1987. "Strategies for Stimulating the Motivation to Learn." *Performance and Instruction* 26, no. 8: 1–7.

Kohn, Alfie. 1993. "Rewards versus Learning: A Response to Paul Chance." *Phi Delta Kappa* 74, no.10 (June): 783–787.

Kolb, David A. 1984. *Experiential Learning: Experience as the Source of Learning and Development.* Upper Saddle River, NJ: Prentice-Hall.

Maslow, Abraham. 1943. "A Theory of Human Motivation." *Psychological Review* 50, no. 4 (July): 370–396. doi:10.1037/h0054346.

Piaget, Jean. 1929. *The Child's Conception of the World.* New York: Routledge; reprinted in 1997.

Seligman, Martin E. P. 1975. *Helplessness: Depression, Development and Death.* New York: W. H. Freeman.

Small, Ruth V. 2005. *Designing Digital Literacy Programs with IM-PACT: Information Motivation, Purpose, Audience, Content, and Technique.* New York: Neal-Schuman.

Small, Ruth V., and Marilyn P. Arnone. 1998/1999. "Arousing and Sustaining Curiosity: Lessons from the ARCS Model." *Training Research Journal* 4, 103–116.

———. 2000. *Turning Kids On to Research: The Power of Motivation.* Englewood, CO: Libraries Unlimited.

Small, Ruth V., Bernie Dodge, and Xi Jiang. 1996. *Dimensions of Interest and Boredom in Instructional Situations.* Proceedings of Selected Research and Development Presentations at the 1996 National Convention of the Association for Educational Communications and Technology: Indianapolis, IN.

Small, Ruth V., and Myke Gluck. 1994. "The Relationship of Motivational Conditions to Effective Instructional Attributes: A Magnitude Scaling Approach." *Educational Technology* 34, no. 8 (October): 33–40.

Summerville, Jennifer B. 1998. *The Role of Awareness of Cognitive Style in Hypermedia.* Proceedings at the National Convention of the Association for Educational Communications and Technology (AECT): St. Louis, MO.

Tomlinson, Carol A. 2000. "Reconcilable Differences? Standards-Based Teaching and Differentiation." *Educational Leadership* 58, no. 1 (September): 6–11.

Weiner, Bernard. 1972. "Attribution Theory, Achievement Motivation, and the Educational Process." *Review of Educational Research* 42, no. 2 (Spring): 203–215.

Witkin, Herman A., C. A. Moore, Donald R. Goodenough, and P. W. Cox. 1977. "Field-Dependent and Field-Independent Cognitive Styles and Their Educational Research Implications." *Review of Educational Research* 47, no. 1: 1–64.

Wlodkowski, Raymond. 1993. *Enhancing Adult Motivation to Learn: A Guide to Improving Instruction and Increasing Learner Achievement.* Hoboken, NJ: Jossey-Bass.

DIGGING DEEPER

Achilles, Charles M. 1997. "Small Classes, Big Possibilities." *The School Administrator*, October: 6–9;12–13, 15.

Deci, Edward L., with Richard Flaste. 1995. *Why We Do What We Do: Understanding Self-Motivation*. New York: Penguin Books.

Dunn, Rita. 1999. "How Do We Teach Them When We Don't Know How They Learn?" *Teaching K–8* 29, no. 7 (April): 50–55.

Keller, John M. 2010. *Motivational Design for Learning and Performance: The ARCS Model Approach*. New York: Springer.

Wlodkowski, Raymond J., and Judith H. Jaynes. 1990. *Eager to Learn: Helping Children Become Motivated and Love Learning*. San Francisco: Jossey-Bass.

For a set of useful tools for lesson planning and digital book creation that meet the needs of students with special needs, visit the Center for Applied Special Technology (CAST) website at http://www.cast.org/learningtools/index .html.

Selecting and Organizing Content

The classroom teacher sends a group of six first and second grade students from her multi-level class to the library to choose books to take back to the classroom for their unit on community helpers. The children will be completing projects in teams in the classroom on their topic. Dan Brown, the librarian, notices a new student in the group—Joey, an eight-year-old child with Down syndrome. Joey can decode simple, individual words but Dan is not sure whether Joey knows how to select a book that he can read to find information about a community helper for his team.

Introduction

In Chapters 2 and 3, you learned that it is essential to consider the goals for your instruction (Purpose) and the characteristics of your learners (Audience), using the information to carefully craft lessons that meet the specific needs and interests of your learners. Once you have completed the analysis of your learning audience, you can turn your attention to the Content of your instruction, specifically how to analyze classroom curriculum content to understand the instructional context, how to align your instruction with the information needs of the students, how to organize your instruction to create dynamic, inquiry-based learning experiences, and how to assess student learning. In the scenario with Joey, you see how important a learner analysis is. In this case, Dan knew the instructional context (community helpers), but he did not know Joey's skill level in locating books on community helpers or in selecting a book that he could read. In fact, Dan suspected that none of the first grade students knew how to select "just-right" (not too easy, not too difficult) information books. Dan also did not know what these first graders were going to do with the information they found (he suspected the students didn't either). Were they creating a class book, presenting in a community helper fair, or simply turning in their notes to the teacher?

Essential Questions

- How does the curriculum context drive the content of the instructional program of the library?
- How can librarians model, teach, and scaffold inquiry skills to enable students to pursue inquiry-based learning independently?
- How can student learning be assessed?

Chapter Outcomes and Indicators

After the completion of Chapter 4 and taking advantage of other learning opportunities on this book's companion website (http://teachingforinquiry.net), you should achieve these learning outcomes and indicators:

1. OUTCOME: Understand how curriculum context is used to determine the content of the library instructional program.
   a. INDICATOR: Analyze the curriculum maps/plans of classroom teachers to determine content areas of focus.
   b. INDICATOR: Connect needed inquiry skills to curriculum areas of focus and sequence.
   c. INDICATOR: Gain a broad understanding of the K–12 continuum of inquiry skills.
2. OUTCOME: Align the content of instruction with information needs of students.
   a. INDICATOR: Analyze the final product the students will be expected to create to determine the required inquiry and information skills.
   b. INDICATOR: Match the type of information for students to gather with the inquiry phase of the learning experience.
   c. INDICATOR: Match the skills to be taught with the inquiry phase of the learning experience and student skill level.
3. OUTCOME: Employ constructivist teaching strategies and organize instruction to enable students to develop and practice the inquiry learning skills content.
   a. INDICATOR: Do a task analysis of the skills to be taught.
   b. INDICATOR: Develop lesson plans that provide direct instruction, guided practice, independent practice, and reflection.
   c. INDICATOR: Use a variety of teaching strategies that engage the students in active learning.
4. OUTCOME: Assess student learning of inquiry skills both during (formative assessment) and at the completion of (summative assessment) an instructional experience.
   a. INDICATOR: Use graphic organizers and other techniques to assess students' understanding of the skills during the instructional experience.
   b. INDICATOR: Integrate the assessment of inquiry skills with the assessment of the content learning in the final product.
   c. INDICATOR: Provide opportunities for students to assess own and others' work.

Determining the content of library instruction to teach inquiry is multifaceted and complex because you need to consider the curriculum context, students' information needs, constructivist teaching strategies, and how students' learning will be assessed. The following sections will help you navigate these considerations to create engaging instruction that teaches students to be active and motivated inquirers for learning.

Alignment of Library Instruction to Curriculum of School

Research in our field is very clear; giving isolated skills instruction with no connection to classroom learning is minimally effective. Unless students have a reason to use information or pursue inquiry, they may complete a library task, but they will not value or remember the skill.

The dilemma that you may be facing is the difficulty of finding time to collaborate with your classroom teachers to find out the curriculum they are teaching. If you are an elementary librarian, you may face the added pressure of scheduled classes throughout the day (if it's Monday, it must be library time) and limited flexible time for classes to pursue in-depth investigations.

The best scenario is that a school or district will have developed curriculum maps for every grade level and every subject area, complete with timelines, essential questions, and suggested final assessment products. You may use these maps to analyze where it would be most appropriate to integrate the teaching of specific inquiry skills, so that your coherent curriculum of information skills is aligned with and embedded in the content curricula. For example, if Dan's first grade teachers have mapped their curriculum to teach "Who am I?" during the fall semester and "What is my community?" during the second semester, Dan can plan to teach skills like self-assessment of reading interests early in the year and asking questions to find information later in the year.

If your school does not have curriculum maps, the new Common Core State Standards may offer a partial solution for you, especially with the increased emphasis on informational reading and writing (which includes research). The overlap of informational reading and writing (research) skills and your inquiry skills curriculum is probably extensive, so your instruction can be aligned with classroom instruction around the Common Core. You offer the added benefit to your teachers of connecting different areas of the curriculum, so that informational reading and inquiry skills instruction in the library can be integrated with social studies or science content.

There is a logical sequence to the development of inquiry skills, both across each year and across the grades. If you do not have a curriculum plan for the teaching of inquiry skills, you might benefit from looking at one from another school or district (see New York City's Information Fluency Continuum at http://schools.nyc.gov/Academics/LibraryServices/Standardsand Curriculum/ as an example). Curriculum plans are, however, just guides because the teaching of inquiry skills must be tailored to your school's specific content-area curricula and the needs of your students.

Matching the content of your inquiry skills instruction with the content of classroom curricula is complex, but it should be approached through high-level planning rather than reactive decision making for each library lesson. Your students will benefit from a strategic and coherent instructional plan that ensures that they learn both the inquiry process and appropriate inquiry skills and that they have repeated opportunities to practice those skills and deepen their understanding. That plan must be developed in collaboration with classroom teachers as they are thinking through their content curriculum maps. The resultant maps should provide an integrated approach to curriculum, guiding the match between instructional content of the classroom and instructional content of the library.

Let's look at a brief example. Imagine that you are a middle school librarian for grades 6–8. The seventh-grade social studies teachers have decided to deepen their students' understanding of American History to 1865 by rewriting their essential questions and rethinking the final products for each unit. Two units during the year lend themselves to in-depth investigations in the library—Colonization/Revolutionary War and Civil War/Reconstruction. In their planning session about the

> **TAKING ACTION**
>
> Although you will not always have the opportunity to participate in curriculum planning with your teachers, you can use the same matching strategy to align your instructional content with what is happening in the classroom. Try developing a matrix to keep track of your instructional content plans, so that you can see how your skills are integrated into all curriculum areas and across the grades.

Revolutionary War unit, the teachers and librarian decide that students will produce flyers, information pieces, and speeches from people representing different points of view in the months leading up to the Revolution. The librarian offers to teach students about point of view—identifying, gathering evidence, and building an argument from one point of view. The inquiry skill, determining point of view, is added to the social studies curriculum map for that unit.

Connecting Library Instructional Content with Student Information Needs

Now, more than ever before, students need to develop the skills to be effective consumers of information. They need to be able to inquire on their own, to understand when information is needed, and to locate, evaluate, and effectively use that information to meet their academic and personal learning goals. College and career readiness rests on a foundation of inquiry learning skills. Certainly, skills form the backbone of the content of library instruction. You, as a librarian, have assumed responsibility for teaching those inquiry learning skills.

The content of library instruction also includes attention to the type of information that students need for different assignments and questions, while building their learning confidence. If students are at an early stage of a unit on ecosystems, for example, they need to understand the *concept* of ecosystem and the *key ideas* that define any ecosystem. Later in their study, students will need more *specific facts* and *evidence* to understand how ecosystems work and how they differ from each other. Even later in the unit, students might need to find *comparative information* to help them place the evidence they've found on their ecosystem into context. Through your instruction, students learn to differentiate among types of information and to select the most appropriate type for their needs.

Finally, when you're deciding the content of your library instruction, you will need to consider the final product that the students are expected to create. For the unit on ecosystems, if the students are expected to produce a "60 Minutes" video documentary on the decline of ecosystems, then you may need to teach students to develop a line of argument with supporting evidence, as well as the production skills of storyboarding and videotaping. If, on the other hand, students are producing travel brochures to entice visitors to visit specific ecosystems, then you may need to teach students to identify main ideas with supporting evidence, to find or create visuals, to write from a point of view, and to create an effective layout.

Consideration of Types of Information and Skills to Teach and Scaffold

The skill of determining appropriate information has become increasingly important for librarians to teach as the volume of information explodes and access turns to the disorganized "Wild West of the Web." Your students are probably not aware of the different types of information available (e.g., everything from facts and definitions to opinions and propaganda to conceptual think pieces), nor have they probably considered the most appropriate type of information for the different phases of inquiry. Where in their inquiry investigation would it be most valuable for them to locate definitions of key terms, for example? Students need to be taught that starting an investigation with clarity about the meaning of the main terms that underlie the inquiry topic will save them many hours of finding irrelevant information.

You can help your students understand the types of information available and the usefulness of various types for different phases of inquiry by *teaching* inquiry in the manner that you want students to *learn* through inquiry—using different types of information in your instruction and aligning them with the inquiry process and skills.

Small and Arnone (2002) have identified three main types of *information elements* that you may include in an instructional experience: core, clarifying, and enriching. All three types of information may be used at each phase of inquiry, and probably most effectively in that order—from core to clarifying to enriching.

Core Information Elements

Core information provides the foundation for any lesson and might also incorporate prerequisite information for review or reteaching in order to build students' confidence and ensure learning success. Core information elements are typically expository statements comprised of facts, concepts, principles, procedures, processes, and/or opinions related to the topic to be investigated or taught (Small and Arnone, 2002). Each of these types of core information elements are discussed in the following sections.

While every lesson must contain at least some core information, if you decide to teach only core information, the result will likely be a boring and lean lesson. Therefore, you might want to consider adding clarifying and enriching information elements.

Clarifying Information Elements

Because inquiry skills are quite abstract and sometimes challenging for students to learn, you need to provide additional information that describes or explains the core information. These types of explanatory elements are called *clarifying information elements* (Small and Arnone, 2002). Clarifying information elements add layers of complexity to core information that help learners more fully understand the core information and become more confident learners (Small and Arnone, 2002). Clarifying information also contributes to making the information more interesting and more understandable for your students. It is useful for gaining and maintaining attention to and providing relevance for your lesson, as well as building students' confidence in their ability to learn information literacy skills. Some examples of clarifying information elements are advance organizers, examples, analogies, definitions, demonstrations, personal anecdotes, summaries, questions, and informative feedback. We'll describe these in more detail later in this chapter.

Enriching Information Elements

Teaching a constructivist lesson that uses an inquiry approach and contains *both* core and clarifying information will certainly have greater learning and motivation outcomes than a lesson with core information alone. However, if you really want your lesson to have an *I+M-PACT* on student learning and motivation, try adding some *enriching information elements*.

Enriching your core and clarifying information will make learning more exciting and memorable for your students (Small and Arnone, 2002). Some enriching information, like testimonials and case studies, may be discovered by students as they dig deeper into their research. You can use other types of enriching information (e.g., attention-focusing devices, mnemonics) (Small and Arnone, 2002) to turn your ordinary lesson into a lesson masterpiece!

It is important to understand which of these information elements you will emphasize in your lesson, because when you assess student learning, you want to make sure you are assessing the appropriate type of information. For example in the case of basic, core information, assessing knowledge of basic facts is very different from assessing understanding of a concept or ability to complete a procedure.

Matching Student Needs for Core and Clarifying Information to Inquiry Phases

Connect

At the beginning of an inquiry project, students have several information needs. They must first have an overall understanding of the ideas that frame their inquiry; in other words, they need background information. For that, students might want to locate information about the concepts that undergird their inquiry topic. Students who are going to do a project on an endangered species, for example, must start with an understanding of what it means to be endangered.

Concepts: A concept is a classification that includes at least two examples that share common characteristics. An example of a concept is primary sources. This is a concept and not a fact because it is possible to cite at least two examples of primary sources. Students who are expected to use primary sources in their research must be able to recognize that type of source and to understand the strengths and limitations that primary sources present.

Definitions: Another important type of information for the Connect phase of inquiry is the definition. Students should know the meaning of key terms relevant to their topic (although they will continue to build this list throughout their research) and understand both the denotation and the connotation of those terms.

An example from practice shows the importance of definitions for students during any inquiry experience, even direct instruction by the librarian. Several years ago, a student intern was teaching a lesson on bibliographies to high school seniors. Throughout her lesson, she used library jargon and acronyms with which she was very familiar but her students hadn't a clue. The faces of those students turned from interest to total confusion to complete boredom. Soon students were doodling, sleeping, talking among themselves, anything but paying attention to the lesson.

Whenever you introduce unfamiliar terms or acronyms to your students, do not make assumptions about what they know. It is essential that you provide definitions for unfamiliar terms to your learning audience, and when you have a large number of unfamiliar terms, you might consider providing a glossary with all potentially unknown terms and definitions. In addition to facilitating learning, this will help increase learning motivation by increasing students' learning confidence and sustaining interest in your lesson. You could also create a system with your students in which they give some type of signal when they encounter an unfamiliar word or phrase. You could stop the lesson and ask students to find the definition in a dictionary or online. The first one to do so reads it to the class. Teaching students to identify concepts and definitions will help them recognize those types of information when they need them for their own research.

Wonder

Questions: Questioning is the heart of inquiry learning. Unfortunately, although teachers often drive their instruction with questions, they may not teach students to ask questions themselves. Students should be encouraged to ask questions of you and each other about whatever seems curious to them or what they don't understand. As we collect data from successful young inventors and entrepreneurs, it is clear that the stimulus for their creativity is wonder; i.e., seeing a problem, wondering how to solve it, and asking lots of questions that provide the kind of information they need to create a solution.

Therefore, it isn't enough to just ask questions. Students need to understand how to ask the *kinds* of questions that will help to clarify their information problem, successfully find needed information, and challenge their thinking. You can help students learn how to ask meaningful questions by modeling their use in your instruction and being explicit about the types of questions you are asking (and why).

Questions are often part of a lesson's content as a check for student learning. Some questions can require simple memorization (e.g., What does nonfiction mean?). But these kinds of questions are of limited value when trying to foster high-level, critical-thinking skills. Therefore, when asking questions of students it is important to:

1. avoid yes/no questions unless you follow up with a "why" or "how" question;
2. make sure the question is clearly stated and understandable (in fact, you might want to restate a complex question in another way or break it up into smaller questions);
3. vary the cognitive level of the questions asked in order to stimulate higher-order thinking skills (application, analysis, synthesis, and evaluation);
4. be an active listener to students' responses; and
5. model good questioning techniques.

Here are some examples of higher cognitive-level inquiry questions for students:

- "Can you identify each of the research skills that you used while completing your research project?" (Analysis)
- "What are different ways in which you can present the information you have gathered?" (Synthesis)
- "For this assignment, what is the best type of resource to use and why?" (Evaluation)

> **TAKING ACTION**
>
> Ask your students to share examples of their inquiry learning outside of school; i.e., what they wonder about when they are home, at the playground, etc. Be sure to ask them to describe what triggered that inquiry. This will give you insight into how to stimulate their interest.

Investigate

Most of students' information needs emerge during the Investigate phase of inquiry, and, indeed, you teach many important investigation skills to help them find and draw meaning from the information they locate. Logically, students will gather core information first, so that they know the basic evidence to answer their research questions. However, students sometimes have difficulty distinguishing between core and clarifying information—they gather large ideas and little details, facts and examples at the same time and with the same level of priority. As a result, they may have trouble identifying the main ideas and organizing their information to form a conclusion.

During instruction, you can model and teach how to use the different types of core information they may find. You can help them understand what a fact is and how a fact differs from an opinion. You can model for them how to use both in their final product. The following examples may help you teach students the different types of information to gather during their investigations.

Facts: A fact is a statement that can have only one example. While an effective instructional presentation is not made up solely of facts, some facts may be included. In a lesson on website addresses, an example of a fact is that the extension *"gov"* refers to a government entity.

You can use facts to stimulate discussions and inquiry, particularly startling facts. For example, posting a list of popular children's and young adult books that have been censored could trigger an active discussion of censorship and intellectual freedom in your library.

Opinions: An opinion is a belief. Just as opinions can be used in research if they are well-founded and identified, you can sometimes appropriately express your opinions during a lesson, especially if that opinion is based on personal knowledge or experience. Of course, you need to be careful to label your statement as *your* opinion. Particularly helpful to students would be showing the facts that led you to form your opinion, so that students can see the linkages between the two forms of information.

An interactive lesson on fact versus opinion might ask students to respond to the results of a public opinion poll by positing the factual evidence that supports each possible response. Students who understand how to use opinions can quote the opinions of experts in their research products and include the validating evidence that the experts have cited. They are also useful when participating in activities such as debates. However, students must also understand that opinion can cross that fine line into bias, when alternative opinions are not represented.

Like facts, some opinions may be included in an instructional presentation but should be used sparingly so as not to impose a particular point of view on your students. Students need to be exposed to differing viewpoints in order to learn to make informed decisions about an issue.

Besides teaching students how to use opinions and evidence from others effectively, you will want to guide students in forming their own opinions based on the evidence that they collect. If you are teaching young children, start by asking them to name their favorite book or author with a justification as to why it is their favorite. You could ask older students to reflect on their research topic and voice their opinion about the importance, impact, causes, or effects, using the facts they have gathered to support their thinking.

Examples: Examples are among the most common type of clarifying information discovered during inquiry investigations. Examples are used to provide concreteness to abstract concepts by describing instances of a particular concept, principle, or procedure. In your instruction, providing familiar examples will increase relevance of the topic for your students. Students who are expected to use primary sources in their research, for example, would benefit greatly from the opportunity to examine a number of primary-source examples. A powerful constructivist lesson on primary sources would have the students develop a definition of primary sources from examples. Where possible, you should have your students provide the examples for each other. Case studies and demonstrations may be thought of as complex examples.

Procedures: When teaching information-seeking skills to students, we often use another information element—procedures—to provide scaffolding. A procedure (aka process) is an ordered set of actions that achieves a goal and may be described or demonstrated as a series of steps. For example, you want students to learn the locating skill of finding a nonfiction book on the shelf. You can provide students with a simple job aid that includes these steps to follow: (1) identify the Dewey number for that book, (2) locate the shelf that holds books with that Dewey number, (3) scan the shelf for books with that Dewey number on their spine, and (4) identify the desired book by checking the title and author's name. As students practice the process, they will begin to internalize it and, soon, no longer need any assistance.

Later in this chapter, we present a process called *task analysis.* Task analysis is a way to plan out procedural content so that it is presented in the most effective and efficient manner. When you read about task analysis, think about the example above and see if we might have omitted any steps that are vital to the procedure of locating a desired nonfiction book on the bookshelf.

Construct

The construct phase of inquiry, when students are expected to construct their own understanding, is perhaps the most difficult for students because many have never been taught how to draw conclusions, synthesize, compare and contrast, or develop a line of argument. Students can find both core and clarifying information that helps them form conclusions and construct their own ideas.

Summaries: The easiest type of construct activity is summarization. A recap is one way to provide a summary of a large set of information presented. Students may be able to locate summaries at the beginning and end of book chapters or articles, but the most powerful summaries are those done by the students themselves. You can teach students to recap, or build a bulleted list of the main points, by pausing periodically in your instruction for students to summarize what they've learned. These periodic summaries will help build students' confidence in their ability to be successful learners. Stopping a lesson at key points and asking a student to provide a brief recap is also one way to make sure students pay attention and listen and also checks understanding.

Analogies: Analogies, another clarifying information element, are comparisons between an abstract, unfamiliar concept and a concrete, familiar one. Analogies are often used when it is difficult to provide an example. For example, you will often find in science textbooks an analogy of electrical current to water flowing through a pipe. It is difficult to demonstrate electrical current but students can easily watch water flow through a pipe. When students make a connection between a new idea and an idea they already understand, then they have a deeper level of understanding than if they just learned a definition or read a description of the new idea. Motivationally, analogies can create interest in a topic and improve learning confidence through greater understanding.

Students can be asked to create their own analogies for certain concepts. One technique that has proven very successful in helping students firm up their conceptual understanding is called synectics, in which students are asked to compare a new concept to an unrelated one. In making the comparisons, students identify the major characteristics in common between the old and new concepts. For example, you could ask students, "How are databases like a gym locker?" They could provide the similarities between databases and gym lockers (e.g., they allow you to group similar items), but also ask students to list differences to ensure they don't carry the analogy too far, citing similarities that aren't there and ultimately causing greater confusion.

Principles: Another thinking skill to be fostered during the construct phase is connecting ideas or forming relationships among ideas. An information element that exemplifies this type of thinking is a principle. A principle demonstrates a change relationship that occurs with regularity. Often, principles are stated as "if . . . then" statements. Students may be expected to draw conclusions about cause and effect, for example. You can use principles in your instruction to help students understand how to form relationships between ideas. For example, a principle related to this chapter is, "If you organize information effectively, your content will be more clearly understood and used." You could motivate students to think about principles by stating the opposite in order to stimulate discussion. For the principle stated previously, you might ask students to state the reverse (e.g., "If you don't organize information effectively, your content will be less understood and used") and discuss what the results of that would be.

Express

Students generally do not seek information during the Express phase of inquiry; however, you can increase their success in creating their final product by offering them models for the type of product they must complete. You have probably already discovered the transformative power of authentic assessment products. Students are more motivated to do higher-quality work when they can express their learning in formats that are connected to real life. You may see high school junior boys willingly donning togas to perform their part of a "Good Morning, Greece" show. Classes will enthusiastically research and create news magazines from medieval times or the 1920s. Every type of communication in the world can offer possibilities for student presentation of research, from résumés on the lives of Revolutionary War figures to tweets from an environmental scientist investigating an oil spill.

In addition to providing information-sharing models with the students, you will probably want to harness the power of technology to encourage collaborative work and to publish student work to a broad audience. Chapter 5 offers a deeper look at using technology for teaching inquiry.

Reflect

Reflective information is an essential part of any inquiry process. Ideally, when you provide feedback to the students on their skill development, you are teaching them to be self-reflective as well. More realistically, however, you will want to encourage students to look reflectively at their own work and at the work of others by providing rubrics and protocols that facilitate such thinking. Several protocols for looking at student work can be adapted for use by students. The essential characteristic is to establish timed rounds of commenting (e.g., round 1—describing what can be seen, round 2—asking clarifying questions, round 3—asking probing questions, round 4—offering a "glow" and "grow"). As a teaching librarian, you may also wish to offer two kinds of feedback: informative and motivational.

Informative feedback: Informative feedback is a type of clarifying information that improves the quality of learning and performance by informing learners about where they are making mistakes or heading in the wrong direction so that they are able to self-correct or change unproductive or ineffective learning behavior. As a "guide on the side," providing students with informative feedback helps them understand what they are doing well, how to improve their work, and how their learning success is directly influenced by the amount and quality of their effort.

Informative feedback provides specific, concise corrective advice to the student. It focuses on targeted actions, not attitudes, and is intended to guide or improve the quality of task performance. For maximum usefulness, informative feedback should be given in private just after the performance has been completed or just before the performance is to be repeated (Tosti, 2011). Here are some examples of informative feedback statements:

- "You will need to be sure to correctly cite the sources you have used in your research paper."

- "This project looks good except for the last two parts, which have left out some information. You'll need to check the assignment to find what you omitted and then put it in."

- "I noticed the last time you had to enlarge a digital photo on the screen, your image ended up distorted. This time, place your cursor on one of the corner squares and hold the shift key down as you enlarge your photo. That way the image will remain in proportion."

Motivational feedback: While informative feedback provides corrective suggestions for improving learning, motivational feedback provides encouragement and reinforcement to bolster student motivation, increase the quantity of positive behaviors, and enrich your lesson's content (Tosti, 2011). When assessing learning or achievement, providing students with public or private encouragement or genuine praise tied to effort as they show progress or attain mastery will help to build their confidence, reinforce desirable behavior, and promote learning satisfaction. Some examples of motivational feedback follow:

- "I see you are working very hard to learn this."

- "I'm so proud of the effort you are putting into this project."

- "You must be very pleased with what you have learned today."

- "You've done an excellent job on this project by including all of the required parts in a creative way. You've really contributed to your group's effort."

Matching Student Needs for Skills with Inquiry Phases

The Office of Library Services in New York City has developed a continuum of inquiry skills for grades K–12 using the framework of the Stripling Inquiry Model. Benchmark skills for the grade-level groupings of K–2, 3–5, 6–8, and 9–12 are included in Table 4.1 (New York School Library System, 2010; see the complete Information Fluency Continuum at http://schools .nyc.gov/Academics/LibraryServices/Standards andCurriculum/).

The Common Core State Standards, adopted by 40 states, place great emphasis on the skills that are embedded in library information fluency continuums like that of New York City. An analysis of the intersection between Common Core standards and inquiry skills taught through the library shows the essential role of instruction around the content of inquiry skills at every grade level, K–12. Table 4.2 provides a sample of the alignment between the library curriculum of inquiry skills and the Common Core.

Table 4.1. New York City Inquiry Benchmark Skills

Inquiry Phase	K–2	3–5	6–8	9–12
Connect	• Connects ideas to own interests. • Shares what is known about the general topic to elicit and make connections to prior knowledge. • Recognizes that questions can be answered by finding information.	• Generates a list of key words for a research-based project with guidance. • Uses sources to acquire background information and brainstorms ideas for further inquiry.	• States and verifies what is known about the problem or question and makes connections to prior knowledge. • Revises the question or problem as needed to arrive at a manageable topic for inquiry.	• Identifies key words, concepts, and synonyms, both stated and implied, for topic and uses them to further research. • Develops a schema or mind map to express the big idea and the relationships among supporting ideas and topics of interest. • Develops and refines the topic, problem, or question independently to arrive at a worthy and manageable topic for inquiry. • Explores problems or questions for which there are multiple answers or no "best" answer.
Wonder	• Asks "I wonder" questions about the research topic.	• Asks questions to clarify topics or details. • Assesses questions to determine which can be answered by simple facts, which cannot be answered, and which would lead to an interesting inquiry. • Predicts answers to inquiry questions based on background knowledge and beginning observation or experience.	• Analyzes and evaluates what is known, observed or experienced to form tentative thesis or hypothesis. • Refines questions to guide the search for different types of information (e.g., overview, big-idea, specific detail, cause and effect, comparison).	• Refines questions to provide a framework for the inquiry and to fulfill the purpose of the research. • Plans inquiry to systematically test hypothesis or to gather evidence to validate thesis.

(Continued)

Table 4.1. New York City Inquiry Benchmark Skills *(Continued)*

Inquiry Phase	K–2	3–5	6–8	9–12
Investigate	• Follows a modeled inquiry process during each visit to the library to do research. • Understands the basic organizational structure of books • Distinguishes between fiction and nonfiction resources. • Distinguishes between fact and opinion. • Finds facts and briefly summarizes them via writing, drawing, or verbalization to answer research • Writes, draws, or verbalizes the main idea and supporting details.	• Identifies the ten major Dewey areas and what main topics are included in each. • Searches the online catalog (author, title, and subject) with assistance to locate materials. • Uses bookmarked websites and selected search engines to find appropriate information. • Uses navigation tools of a website to find information. • Paraphrases, summarizes information that answers research questions. • Selects and uses multiple appropriate print, nonprint, electronic, and human sources to answer questions. • Evaluates print and electronic information for usefulness, relevance, and accuracy. • Uses various notetaking strategies.	• Uses online catalog independently to locate specific books, get classification numbers, and browse the shelves. • Uses both primary and secondary sources. • Evaluates quality of electronic and print information for usefulness, currency, authority, and accuracy. • Uses both facts and opinions responsibly by identifying and verifying them. • Uses different formats (e.g., books, websites, subscription databases, multimedia, graphs, charts, maps, and diagrams) as sources of information. • Recognizes the effect of different perspectives and points of view on information. • Recognizes that own point of view influences the interpretation of information.	• Conducts advanced web searches using Boolean logic and other sophisticated search functions. • Uses the organizational features of a book as well as abstracts, tables, charts, and first and last chapters to locate main ideas, specific supporting evidence, and a balanced perspective. • Takes notes using one or more of a variety of note-taking strategies, including reflecting on the information (e.g., graphic organizers, two-column notes). • Pursues a balanced perspective by evaluating information based on authority, accuracy, point of view, and reliability. • Challenges ideas in text and makes notes of questions to pursue in additional sources.
Construct	• Demonstrates simple organizational skills such as sorting and categorizing. • Draws a conclusion about the main idea with guidance.	• States the main idea. • Identifies facts and details that support main ideas. • Uses common organizational patterns (chronological order, main idea with supporting details) to organize information.	• Combines information and weighs evidence to draw conclusions and create meaning. • Uses common organizational patterns (chronological order, cause and effect, compare/contrast) to organize information in order to draw conclusions.	• Organizes information independently, deciding the structure based on the relationships among ideas and general patterns discovered. • Draws clear and appropriate conclusions supported by evidence and examples.

(Continued)

Table 4.1. New York City Inquiry Benchmark Skills (Continued)

Inquiry Phase	K–2	3–5	6–8	9–12
Construct (*Continued*)	• Compares new ideas with what was known at the beginning of the inquiry.	• Forms opinion and uses evidence from text to back it up.	• Interprets information and ideas by defining, classifying, and inferring. • Draws conclusions based on explicit and implied information.	• Presents different perspectives with evidence for each. • Develops own point of view and supports with evidence. • Builds a conceptual framework by synthesizing ideas gathered from multiple sources.
Express	• Presents facts and simple answers to questions. • Presents information in a variety of ways (e.g., art, music, poetry, movement, verbally, and/or written language).	• Chooses the format for the product based on personal preference or uses format chosen by the teacher or librarian. • Cites all sources used according to model provided by teacher. • Modifies and revises own work based on feedback from teachers and others. • Presents information clearly so that main points are evident.	• Presents conclusions and supporting facts in a variety of ways • Cites all sources used according to local style formats. • Creates products for authentic reasons and audiences.	• Cites all sources used according to standard style formats. • Chooses the most appropriate format, tone, and language to communicate ideas clearly in real-world formats to different audiences. • Evaluates own product and process throughout the work and uses self-assessment, teacher feedback, and peer feedback to make revisions when necessary.
Reflect	• Identifies own strengths and sets goals for improvement. • Asks, "What do I wonder about now?"	• Chooses the format for the product based on personal preference or uses format chosen by the teacher or librarian. • Cites all sources used according to model provided by teacher. • Modifies and revises own work based on feedback. • Presents information clearly so that main points are evident.	• Identifies own strengths and sets goals for improvement. • Uses established criteria or collaborates with classmates and teacher to develop criteria for assessment.	• Identifies own strengths and sets goals for improvement. • Records individual experience of the inquiry process—the hardest part, best part, skills learned, insights experienced, etc.—with suggestions for future improvements.

Table 4.2. Inquiry Skills/Common Core Alignment

Grade 3

Common Core Standards for English Language Arts

Reading Standards for Literature

- Connects ideas in texts to own interests.
- States what is known about the problem or question and makes connections to prior knowledge.
- Questions text during reading or listening.
- Uses a variety of strategies to determine important ideas.
- **States the main idea [Assessment available].**
- Selects both "just right" materials and challenging materials on a regular basis.
- Begins to explore and examine the various genres based on personal interests.

Reading Standards for Informational Text

- Connects ideas in texts to own interests.
- States what is known about the problem or question and makes connections to prior knowledge.
- Formulates questions about the topic with guidance.
- Locates nonfiction material at appropriate reading level.
- **Searches the online catalog (author, title, and subject) with assistance to locate materials [Assessment available].**
- **Uses bookmarked websites to find appropriate information [Assessment available].**
- Selects and uses multiple appropriate print, nonprint, electronic, and human sources to answer questions.
- Uses at least two sources for research projects.
- Questions text during reading or listening.
- Identifies and uses the organizational structures of a nonfiction book to locate information.
- Uses a variety of strategies to determine important ideas.
- **States the main idea [Assessment available].**
- Selects both "just right" materials and challenging materials on a regular basis.
- Gathers information related to personal interests.
- Begins to explore and examine the various genres based on personal interests.

Reading Standards: Foundational Skills

- Foundational skills are taught in the classroom and reinforced in the library.

Writing Standards

- Uses prior knowledge and understanding of overall topic to make predictions about what the new information will reveal.
- Formulates questions about the topic with guidance.
- Uses simple note-taking strategies.
- Organizes information using a teacher-provided tool.
- Communicates new understandings through combining, predicting, illustrating, and constructing.
- Identifies and evaluates the important features for a good product.

(Continued)

Table 4.2. Inquiry Skills/Common Core Alignment (Continued)

Grade 3 (Continued)

Common Core Standards for English Language Arts

Writing Standards (Continued)

- **Chooses the format for the product based on personal preferences or uses format chosen by the teacher or librarian [Assessment available].**
- **Presents information clearly so that main points are evident [Assessment available].**
- Uses visuals and multimedia to communicate meaning.
- **Assesses and revises own work with guidance [Assessment available].**
- Gathers information related to personal interests.

Speaking and Listening Standards

- Formulates questions about the topic with guidance.
- Questions text during reading or listening.
- Communicates new understandings through combining, predicting, illustrating, and constructing.
- Uses visuals and multimedia to communicate meaning.
- Identifies and evaluates the important features for a good product.
- Asks "What about this topic would I like to learn more about?"
- Discusses problems and solutions in a work.
- Shows respect for and responds to the ideas of others.

Language Standards

- Language skills are taught in the classroom and reinforced in the library.

Additional Information Fluency Skills Taught through the Library

- **Identifies the ten major Dewey areas and what main topics are included in each [Assessment available].**
- **Identifies own strengths and sets goals for improvement [Assessment available].**
- Demonstrates responsibility and awareness that library resources are to be shared among the entire school community.
- Observes Internet safety procedures, including safeguarding personal information.
- Digital Citizenship
  - Safety: Respecting the privacy of others
  - Responsibility: Safe Searching—staying in a kid-friendly zone and what to do when things go wrong

Grade 7

Common Core Standards for English Language Arts

Reading Standards for Literature

- Recognizes the creator's point of view; recognizes that there are diverse points of view that lead to different insights.
- Participates in literary discussions and book clubs.
- Independently locates and selects information for personal, hobby, or vocational interests.

(Continued)

Table 4.2. Inquiry Skills/Common Core Alignment *(Continued)*

Grade 7 *(Continued)*

Common Core Standards for English Language Arts

Reading Standards for Literature *(Continued)*

- Reads independently.
- Selects print and nonprint materials based on personal interests, knowledge of authors, and reading level.

Reading Standards for Informational Text

- Determines what resources will most likely offer quality information.
- Uses table of contents, index, chapter and section headings, topic sentences, and summary sentences to locate information and select main ideas.
- **Evaluates quality of electronic and print information for usefulness, currency, authority, and accuracy [Assessment available].**
- Recognizes the creator's point of view; recognizes that there are diverse points of view that lead to different insights.
- **Uses both facts and opinions responsibly by identifying and verifying them [Assessment available].**
- **Interprets information and ideas by defining, classifying, and inferring.**
- Questions the differences between sources and seeks additional sources to resolve.
- Forms opinions and judgments backed up by supporting evidence.
- Independently locates and selects information for personal, hobby, or vocational interests.
- Reads independently.
- Selects print and nonprint materials based on personal interests, knowledge of authors, and reading level.
- Considers culturally divergent and opposing viewpoints on topics.

Writing Standards

- **States and verifies what is known about the problem or question and makes connections to prior knowledge [Assessment available].**
- Uses multiple sources to acquire background information and brainstorms ideas for further inquiry.
- Writes questions independently based on key ideas or areas of focus.
- **Analyzes and evaluates what is known, observed, or experienced to form tentative thesis or hypothesis [Assessment available].**
- Determines what resources will most likely offer quality information.
- Considers culturally divergent and opposing viewpoints on topics.
- Uses the categorization of materials within Dewey areas to locate resources and browse for additional materials.
- Uses technology resources such as online encyclopedias, online databases, and web subject directories to locate information on assigned topics in the curriculum.
- Uses organizational systems and electronic search strategies (keywords, subject headings) to locate appropriate resources.
- Questions the differences between sources and seeks additional sources to resolve.
- Uses table of contents, index, chapter and section headings, topic sentences, and summary sentences to locate information and select main ideas.
- Uses the structure and navigation tools of a website to find the most relevant information.

(Continued)

Table 4.2. Inquiry Skills/Common Core Alignment *(Continued)*
Grade 7 *(Continued)*
Common Core Standards for English Language Arts

Writing Standards *(Continued)*

- Evaluates and paraphrases information that answers research questions.
- **Evaluates quality of electronic and print information for usefulness, currency, authority, and accuracy [Assessment available].**
- **Uses both facts and opinions responsibly by identifying and verifying them [Assessment available].**
- Takes notes by paraphrasing or using quotation marks when using someone else's words.
- **Interprets information and ideas by defining, classifying, and inferring [Assessment available].**
- **Uses common organizational patterns to organize information in order to draw conclusions [Assessment available].**
- Forms opinions and judgments backed up by supporting evidence.
- Cites all sources used according to local style formats [Assessment available].
- Publishes final product for a particular audience and purpose.

Speaking and Listening Standards

- Publishes final product for a particular audience and purpose.
- Participates in literary discussions and book clubs.

Language Standards

- Language skills are taught in the classroom and reinforced in the library.

Additional Information Fluency Skills Taught through the Library

- **Uses established criteria or collaborates with classmates and teacher to develop criteria for assessment [Assessment available].**
- Discusses security, piracy, and downloading related to safe and responsible use of information and communication technology.
- Uses programs and Internet sites responsibly, efficiently, and ethically.
- Observes Internet safety procedures, including safeguarding personal information and equipment.
- Practices Digital Citizenship skills:
  - Safety: Cyberbullying and responsibility for self
  - Responsibility: Fair use/respecting the digital privacy of yourself and others

Source: **Information skills listed in this table are the Grade-Level Benchmark Skills from the** *New York City Information Fluency Continuum,* http://schools.nyc.gov/Academics/LibraryServices/StandardsandCurriculum/.

Teaching with Enriching Information Elements

Enriching information elements are generally not discovered by students doing their research. Instead, you can use these elements in your teaching to enhance student understanding and increase student engagement. Enriching elements contribute to the *art of teaching*. Enriching element strategies are described briefly in the following text.

Advance Organizers

An advance organizer consists of introductory material presented ahead of the learning task that is at a higher level of abstraction than the learning task itself. Its purpose is to explain, integrate, and interrelate the learning task with previously learned material. At the beginning of each chapter in this book, you have seen a brief scenario used as an advance organizer and intended to provide a conceptual framework for and introduction to the chapter's content.

Advance organizers, first conceived by David Ausubel (e.g., 1978), are teaching tools that foster active learning by providing the learner with an introduction before the learning task is undertaken (Joyce and Weil, 2000). The advance organizer provides an overview of the main concepts to be learned, to which specific new, detailed ideas can later be added as new information is discovered. Many advance organizers are visual in nature (such as a web), so it is easy to draw connections between the starting ideas and new ones. Once learning has been completed, students can analyze the relationships between the advance organizer and the new information. Developing advance organizers to help organize the presentation of information in learning products (e.g., papers, projects, oral presentations) is an excellent skill for students.

Some examples of advance organizers are outlines, concept maps, flowcharts, and graphic organizers. It's important to match the advance organizer with the type of information to be presented. You can model that matching for your students in your use of advance organizers for instruction. For example, if you are teaching students to find a narrow topic that relates to an essential question or concept, you might want to do a con-cept map or web. You can demonstrate how to branch out from each node of the web to more specific ideas, until students find a specific topic that interests them and they can see the relation-ship with the overall question or concept. A flowchart might be the best advance organizer for a chronological presentation about an event; an outline might be best for an essay with a main idea and three supporting points.

> **STOP! THINK! DO!**
>
> Some people think that advance organizers are only useful with older students. Can you suggest an example of a way to use an advance organizer with elementary students?

Attention-Focusing Devices

Attention-focusing devices are particularly useful in learning materials (print, media, electronic) and can be used to direct students' attention to essential core information. In face-to-face instruction, a change in your voice volume, tone, or pitch, a pause in speaking just before introducing the important information, or using verbal phrases like "Now, pay attention because this is really important" are examples of attention-focusing devices. Some ways to focus attention on essential information in text, media, or online are arrows, highlighting, color, and graphics. Motivationally, these help to gain and sustain attention.

Mnemonics

While we want to emphasize higher-order thinking skills, research shows that memorization activities help students learn and retain factual information that forms the basis of higher understanding and critical thought (Finn, 1987). When wondering how many days in a particular month, do you quickly run through the old rhyme *Thirty days hath September, April, June, and November* in your head?

You probably learned these songs, rhymes, acronyms, and jingles as a child and still recall and use them from time to time. They are examples of mnemonics, i.e., memory devices for creating associations. These mnemonics specifically help us remember things like how many days in each month, the notes on the treble clef, the names of the five Great Lakes, the letters in the alphabet, the layers of the earth's atmosphere, the colors of the rainbow, and so on. Rhyme or song mnemonics are particularly effective with young children.

There are several types of mnemonics. An acronym mnemonic consists of a word that uses the first letters of the words on the list. A phrase mnemonic involves developing a memorable sentence where the first letters of each word correspond to the first letter of each word on the list. One colleague uses the memorable phrase "Or is more" when he teaches Boolean logic to graduate library and information science students.

In their book on memory techniques, Lorayne and Lucas (1974) describe chunking mnemonics and elaboration mnemonics. Chunking mnemonics break large groups of information into smaller categories. For example, if we want students to remember a large list of children's fiction authors, we might break the list into those who writes mysteries, historical fiction, fantasy, and realistic fiction.

Elaboration mnemonics are those in which we create visual imagery or stories to help remember long lists of information. For example, to remember the meaning of the Dewey numbers on the library shelf, we could have students imagine a large number "1" lying on a therapist's couch (psychology is the 100s) or a giant praying "2" (religion in the 200s), etc.

> ### STOP! THINK! DO!
>
> Can you think of a song or rhyming mnemonic, incorporating a range of information resources, for accomplishing Indicator 1.2.3: Demonstrate creativity by using multiple resources and formats?

While *you* can spend time developing mnemonics for students to use, you might want to try letting *students* construct their own mnemonics. For example, they could come up with a mnemonic sentence or change the lyrics to a popular song to help them remember the general categories of the Dewey Decimal System. They will enjoy the process and find their mnemonics more relevant and memorable, leading to greater learning satisfaction.

Testimonials

A powerful way to provide relevance and enrich instructional content is through the use of testimonials. Testimonials should describe how the learning helped a person improve his or her life in some way. For example, you could relate how you used information problem-solving skills to solve a personal dilemma. Or, you could invite high school students to visit your library when the eighth graders are there and describe how the skills they learned in middle school have helped them be successful in high school assignments and projects. You could also have some students in the group you are teaching share testimonials with each other about how they are using the skills they are learning at home and at school. Testimonials help the learning seem more relevant and important to students.

Case Studies

Whether it is deciding what to wear to the prom or which resources to use for a science project, students encounter information problems on a daily basis. These twenty-first-century learning skills are essential for solving information problems in school and in their personal lives. Case studies use a story-like format to present lesson concepts and principles and provide authentic, thought-provoking, carefully conceived but ill-structured problems to which students apply those concepts and principles in order to solve those problems and make decisions (e.g., the Harry and Sally case study throughout this book).

Problem-based learning is at the heart of inquiry learning, putting students in an active learning role as creative problem solvers confronted with real-world problems. These problems typically have a range of solutions; students must use a variety of information resources to seek out new information and integrate it with current knowledge to develop solutions. Motivationally speaking, these problems must (1) be relevant, requiring students to invoke prior knowledge and experience, (2) be challenging, and force students to think in new and different ways, (3) require the use of multiple resources, (4) provide opportunities for cooperative group learning, and (5) offer authentic learning experiences, transferable to future problems. You may have noticed that we use a problem-based learning approach in this book in the form of our running case study, using the chapter episodes to reinforce the information presented and stimulate *your* inquiry learning skills.

Other Factors to Consider in Determining Content of Instruction

As you select the core, clarifying, and enriching information essential to meeting your instructional goals, there are some other factors to consider, including the *quality* of the information, the *amount and scope* of information to include, and the *form* in which the information is presented. (These are factors that you also can teach your students to consider when they are creating an information presentation or product.)

Quality of Information

In addition to evaluating information *resources*, it is essential that students learn how to evaluate the information they find *within those sources*. Robert Taylor's Value-Added Model (1986) offers a set of critical information quality characteristics for students to learn to use (these characteristics align nicely with 1.1.5: Evaluate information found in selected sources on the basis of accuracy, validity, appropriateness for needs, importance, and social and cultural context).

The following quality characteristics are also useful for you when planning your instruction.

Simplicity: As you determine what and how many clarifying and enriching information elements to include in your lesson, remember to keep it simple, making sure that each element adds learning or motivational value to your lesson. Avoid extraneous or superfluous information.

Accuracy: While it may seem like a no-brainer to the readers of this book, make sure that the information taught and learned is accurate and up-to-date.

Credibility: Be sure the information taught and learned comes from a credible source. With the enormous and ever-increasing amount of information available to us today, credibility becomes an even more essential factor to consider when planning your lesson's content.

Comprehensiveness: If critical core information is left out of your lesson or there is inadequate clarifying and enriching information, your learning audience will likely become confused and dissatisfied and your lesson will seem incomplete. (For some ways to ensure that nothing is missing, see the sections on concept maps and task analysis later in this chapter.)

Usefulness: Information for teaching and learning should be relevant to appropriate curricula and national, state, and local standards and/or to learners' needs and interests. Of course, information intended to motivate students is also useful.

Appropriateness: The level on which you present content should match the learning capability of your learners. For example, if you need to include vocabulary or terms that are unfamiliar to your target learning audience, either begin with more familiar synonyms or define the unfamiliar terms for students. For example, the levels of Bloom's Taxonomy of the content in an online learning module should be matched by the level of assessment for that module.

Amount and Scope of Information

Because librarians are often limited to specific time periods for working with students, they must plan their lessons to be not only effective but also efficient. One of the questions we often hear from pre-service librarians is, "How do you know *how much* information to include in a lesson?" Your stated goals and audience analysis help guide this decision. For example, you might want to have a smaller amount of core information if the content is particularly abstract or difficult or if your learners are at the beginning of the learning process or if you have a mix of student levels. You may choose to include several clarifying information elements if your subject matter is particularly unfamiliar, difficult, or abstract for your learning audience. On the other hand, you might choose a large amount of core information and some clarifying information if the content is relatively easy to learn. If your learners are particularly capable or already know a lot about the topic, you might want to add several enriching elements to maintain their interest and increase participation.

You will also need to decide on the scope (breadth and depth) of information to include. For instance, you may want to focus on one of the *Standards for the 21st-Century Learner* (e.g., Standard 1: Inquire, think critically, and gain knowledge) and just two of the skills (e.g., 1.1.3: Develop and refine a range of questions to frame the search for new understanding and 1.1.4: Find, evaluate, and select appropriate sources to answer questions). You may want to begin your instruction with a broad overview of the entire research process and then focus on the two specific skills, demonstrating where they fit within the process. In this case, you might include a large amount of core information with only a few clarifying and enriching information elements, providing some examples as clarifying information and some enriching information for interest. The amount and scope of content, again, is determined on the basis of the purpose of your instruction and the characteristics of your learning audience.

Form and Design of Information

There are a number of forms that your instructional content can take. The careful consideration of a broad range of student abilities and disabilities, as well as other characteristics that affect learning, is essential to creating inclusive learning programs (e.g., Burgstahler, 2008), including library programs. Universal Design (UD) and Universal Design for Learning (UDL) provide school library media specialists with a framework for designing instruction that meets the range of student needs and abilities (CAST, 2011; Rose and Meyer, 2002).

Applying UDL principles to library and information skills instruction requires multiple representations of the same information (Rose and Meyer, 2002), differentiating the way students can express their learning, and using multiple ways to engage and motivate students (CAST,

2011). For example, you can project information on a screen, but also include an oral description of what is projected visually. In this example, the verbal description has obvious benefits to students with visual impairments, but may also help other students in the class whose learning style is learning by listening (Parker, 2007). The scenario at the beginning of this chapter describes a situation in which school librarians must have at their disposal multiple ways to accommodate a variety of abilities in order to ensure that all students can participate in library activities and make use of the critical information resources already at their disposal (Small, Snyder, and Parker, 2009). Being involved in developing individualized education programs (IEPs) for students with disabilities is an important first step. Application of UDL principles of multiple representation when designing instruction is also essential to meet the needs of all students. In this chapter's example, Dan must help Joey find information that aligns with his skills and needs for meeting the requirements of the learning task. Here are some of the alternative forms that information can take.

Text information: Text (oral or written) information is typically the most common type of information form used in instructional presentations. Text information includes both oral and written information. Some examples of instruction that consists mainly of text information are a lecture, a training manual, a brainstorming session, a textbook, a discussion, and a handout.

Instructional presentations frequently include some combination of text and one or more alternative content forms. These alternative content forms often serve as clarifying or enriching information for your lesson, while at the same time satisfying a variety of learning styles. These include numerical, visual, audio, multimedia, and nonverbal information.

Numerical information: Numbers can add credibility to and increase interest in your content. The use of statistics or numerical facts can substantiate and enrich a fact or opinion. It can also make your lesson more motivating. For example, using a website evaluation instrument that requires students to tally and plot scores on graphs is another example of how numerical information can be useful for helping students learn how to assess the web resources they use for research projects and assignments and for stimulating interest in learning.

Visual information: It is hard to think of a day without encountering some sort of visual information. Whether it's a green light and graphic of a person walking used as a cue to cross a busy city street, a billboard along the highway that conveys a quick warning about the dangers of smoking, or the posters in the library of famous people holding their favorite book, visual information is used to convey important messages to others and to make information more interesting.

There are so many easy methods, such as computer graphics programs and digital cameras, for today's school librarians to capture and display visual information. You might use visual information to convey an online search strategy (graphics), to showcase an exemplary project (photograph), to provide humor through a cartoon (drawing), or to demonstrate the research process to a student research team (video). Of course, you may also use combinations of these forms (e.g., video with titles and closed captioning).

> ### WORDS OF WISDOM
>
> One more subtle and abstract form of content is you, the instructor. Be aware that your posture, stance, facial expressions, gestures, and tone of voice all convey information to your students.

Audio information: As with the other content forms, audio information conveyed through such media as CDs can be used to contribute to the overall message of the instructional presentation by clarifying or enriching the core information. Audio information is most effective in lessons where listening is essential to understanding the core information. For example, listening to an audiotape of a speech by a long-ago president or listening to a story read by its author can add value to learning through voice and dramatic elements that simple text on a page just can't communicate. In some cases the audio can be even more powerful if it is part of a video, allowing students to combine both visual and auditory information to learn.

CHECKPOINT

Selecting content for teaching and learning requires several decisions and considerations, including the types, quality, amount, and scope of information you choose. Your instructional content decisions provide a model for students' use of information during their own inquiry investigations. In addition, determining what content forms you will use can have a major impact on student learning and motivation.

Multimedia information: Multimedia presentations have become commonplace tools in instructional episodes. Technology allows both you and your students to create and shape instructional and learning experiences. Computer-based multimedia, whether on the web or as stand-alone presentation software, incorporate information in two or more formats—text, sound, and/or visual. The Internet, and specifically the web, is filled with information but not all of that information meets Taylor's quality criteria, as well as the other factors. Content forms are a particularly important consideration for meeting the learning style needs of your students and for teaching them visual and media literacy skills (e.g., 2.1.6: Use the writing process, media and visual literacy, and technology skills to create products that express new understandings). The media for delivering these different forms of information are discussed in greater depth in Chapter 5.

Organizing Content for Teaching and Learning Twenty-First-Century Skills

Once you have selected all of the content you want to include in your lesson, you need to organize and sequence it. Constructivist learning theorists emphasize the importance of creating a structure for instruction so that it can be easily understood by students. The lesson framework that many teachers use to provide both direct instruction and student practice has four main segments: direct instruction, modeling and guided practice, independent practice, and sharing and reflecting. The direct instruction is often preceded by a "hook," a motivational introduction to the lesson.

The Introductory Hook

The introduction is intended to give students (1) a brief overview of the goals of the lesson, (2) benefits of the lesson for them, and (3) a feeling of rapport with you as a teacher and fellow learner. Your introduction needs to be interesting and attention-grabbing. Small and Arnone (2002) refer to this as the "hook" of your presentation, used to pique your students' curiosity about and interest in the subject matter (either the curriculum content or the inquiry-skills content) and make it meaningful for them. A hook can gain students' attention by injecting novelty, surprise, or mystery into your lesson. Showing a "trigger" video (one that just introduces an interesting concept), sponsoring a surprise guest speaker, or playing a CD with mysterious sounds when students enter the library are examples of hooks that can be used to stimulate students' curiosity and interest at the beginning of a lesson. Here are some other examples:

- Pose an intriguing or perplexing problem or question to stimulate inquiry.
- Place in plain sight a mystery box or bag with question marks all over it. In the box or bag put small strips of paper with research topics or research sources on each.

- Provide a "sneak preview" to the content of your lesson.
- Dress in a costume or wear a hat that relates to the lesson.
- Project a humorous cartoon.

Direct Instruction

As you move into your mini-lesson of direct instruction, make sure you provide a smooth transition from your introduction, through what Small and Arnone (2002) call a *bridge*. A bridge is a connecting statement or activity that leads the learner seamlessly to the main portion of your lesson.

Selecting the content of the mini-lesson is a critical and complex process that takes into consideration all the factors previously explained in this book—inquiry, motivation, purpose, audience, and content. Even after all those requirements have been taken into account, and you have decided the overall focus of the lesson, you may struggle to pare down the content into a size or complexity that students can successfully learn and practice during the time you have with them. Ideally, this lesson will build on previous lessons and will be continued by ensuing instruction. Practically though, you may have to boil a skill down to its essence because you have only one opportunity to teach it to these particular students.

The way you sequence the body of your mini-lesson is critical for effective teaching. One rule of thumb is this: when teaching subject matter that is particularly difficult, complex, or abstract be sure to begin with simple content and progress to that which is more difficult and complex; start with concrete concepts before introducing more abstract ones.

Two tools may help you identify the specific content you plan to teach and organize the mini-lesson. The first one, *concept mapping*, is useful for knowledge teaching; the other, *task analysis*, is best used with skill teaching. Both methods are also useful for determining if you have selected all of the important information you need for your lesson's content and how that information is interrelated.

Concept mapping: One method for organizing conceptual content is the concept map. A concept map graphically represents all of the concepts to be taught and *their relationships to each other*.

Figure 4.1 illustrates what a concept map might look like. The main concept is presented in the center of a piece of paper or screen by a circle with the term(s) within it. Each related term is represented in a circle drawn around the main concept and connected by lines. Additional lines are drawn connecting related terms where appropriate. There are some excellent concept map creators available on the web to help make concept mapping fun and easy, even for children.

By developing a concept map of your overall focus, you will be able to see the particular aspects that you want to include in your lesson. Sharing the concept map with your students will enable them to put the day's lesson in the context of a larger body of knowledge and the inquiry process. For example, suppose that your students are getting ready to research genetic diseases. You want them to use up-to-date and accurate information, so you plan to teach them about online databases and how to access and search your health database. You develop a concept map of all the resource selections that are possible, organized by currency and level of authority. Students will quickly be able to see why a health database would be the best choice for their research. The concept map has also enabled you to see that a next lesson might focus on another aspect of the resource concept map, like evaluating the authority of a website.

Figure 4.1. Example of a Concept Map

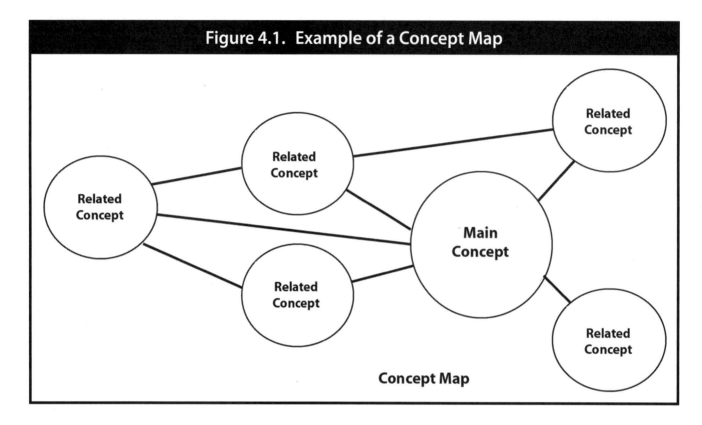

Concept Map

Task analysis: Have you ever had to assemble a child's swing set or follow the manual for a new computer program and become totally lost when you discovered that the directions had left out one or more essential steps in the process? Every day we perform a number of ordinary tasks almost automatically without ever thinking about the complexity of the behaviors they require.

Placing a phone call, making a pizza, doing the laundry, brushing your teeth, and mowing the lawn are all complex tasks that require us to follow a series of steps strung together in pretty much the same way each time in order to be successful. While we may not all perform exactly the same steps to accomplish the task (e.g., you may like different veggies on your pizza while I may prefer plain cheese pizza) or we may perform the same steps but not in the exact same sequence (e.g., you may mow your back yard first while I may prefer to start with my front yard), we are all completing the same basic process with essentially the same results.

Task analysis is a way of sequencing procedural content or processes (skills) by identifying all of the steps needed to accomplish a task and achieve a meaningful outcome; a step represents one of the actions that needs to be taken to reach that desired outcome. While there may be some leeway for ordering some steps (like the example of starting your mowing in the front or back yard), most steps in the process have a logical sequence to follow in order to successfully complete the task. You can make a list of the steps or use a flowchart to document all of the steps in the process. The latter is preferable when you anticipate having decision points and desired repetition during the process.

A task analysis is an important activity as you plan your lesson because it (1) requires you to recognize the complexity of most tasks you require students to perform and (2) helps prevent

TAKING ACTION

If your lesson is mainly conceptual in nature, try developing a concept map of the information you will include. If your lesson is mainly procedural in nature, try performing a task analysis and creating a flowchart of the information you will include.

skipping or inaccurately sequencing important steps in your instructional presentation. The best way to identify each step in the process to be learned is to actually perform the task yourself, recording each of the required steps as you do it. You will likely be amazed at some of the minor steps that you do automatically and take for granted but are essential in the process. If you do not actually perform the task as you develop your task analysis, it is almost guaranteed that you will omit some of these critical steps and doom your lesson to failure.

Many librarians have discovered that the more familiar they are with inquiry, the more important a task analysis becomes, because it is easy to overlook a step that is performed automatically by the experienced investigator. For example, one librarian was trying to help students locate primary-source documents for a history assignment. She finally realized that students were having trouble because they didn't know what a "document" was and they naturally defaulted to selecting websites they found through a Google search.

A task analysis is most commonly represented in flowchart form. Rectangles represent each of the steps in the process; circles represent the start and end of the process; diamonds represent decision points that can return you to a previous step. Figure 4.2 presents a task analysis for a task analysis (don't you hate it when people do that?). For procedural or skill-based content, a task analysis will provide you with a framework for sequencing your lesson.

Modeling and Guided Practice

Once you have taught the main concepts or steps to a process, you need to clarify and enrich your students' understanding by modeling how the skill or process would be applied to a real example. For the primary-source document example above, once you have taught the characteristics of primary sources and documents, you might engage the students in a whole-class analysis of three to four online sources to select the best primary-source documents for the topic. The class discussion should enable all students to clarify their understanding.

Independent Practice

During this phase of the lesson, you give the students a task to complete in pairs or individually that requires that they apply the skill or process they just learned and practiced as a class. An important part of this phase is to build in an expectation that students will capture their work for later sharing with the class or

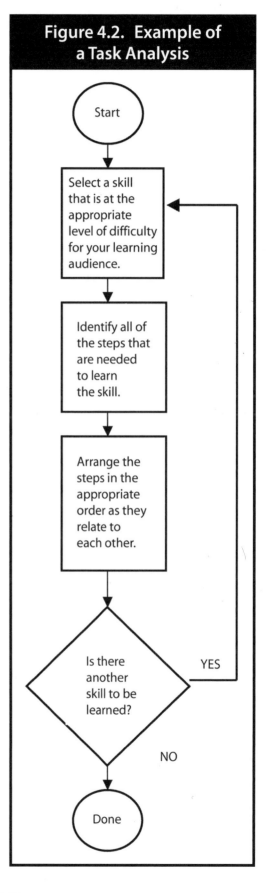

Figure 4.2. Example of a Task Analysis

with you. You can use this student work as formative assessment to determine how well students understood the main ideas of the lesson. See the next section on Assessment for additional information about formative assessment.

Sharing and Reflection

In the best-case scenario, you will have enough time to bring the students back together as a class to share their insights with the class and reflect on how they can use this skill or process in the future. Students may have questions or concerns that you can answer. Your lesson's conclusion needs to be as dynamic as your introduction. You want your students to complete their learning experience with feelings of satisfaction and a desire to learn more. Here are a few more ideas to make sure you have a power ending; perhaps you have some of your own ideas to add to the list.

- Provide a recap or summary of key ideas.
- Allow time for Q&A.
- Give students a chance to demonstrate what they have learned.
- Provide students with additional learning opportunities after the formal lesson has ended.

Assessment of Student Learning

You may want to use both formative and summative assessment as a part of your instruction. Formative assessment is done at key points during the lesson to verify that students are on track with their learning. This may be as simple as asking a few questions or more formal using a brief quiz format.

Summative assessments demonstrate a comprehensive synthesis of what has been learned. The summative assessment product may be determined by the classroom teacher, but you may be able to collaborate during your planning sessions to design the final assessment product together. Previously in this chapter, we have discussed the value of authenticity in motivating students to apply themselves to creating a high-quality product. You don't have to sacrifice reading, writing, and intellectual rigor to offer a product choice that has real-world applications. Students will understand Benjamin Franklin's contributions even better if they prepare a résumé and job application for him, rather than a more traditional (and often less motivating) report.

One of the considerations in designing the final product is the level of thinking and depth of inquiry required by the assignment. Students who are given a brief amount of time to find information about a broad topic or research question cannot be expected to create products with a high degree of synthesis or analysis. A taxonomy of research reactions, called the REACTS Taxonomy, was developed by Barbara Stripling and Judy Pitts (Stripling and Pitts, 1988) and later refined by Stripling and posted online at http://schools.nyc.gov/Academics/Library Services/EducatorResources/ProgramPlanning/.

You may find that the final product evaluation (perhaps guided by a rubric) includes only an assessment of the curriculum content learning, and not an assessment of the inquiry or information skills that you taught. You can work with the teacher to build in an evaluation of those skills and design the product to make some of the skills transparent (and thus assessable). For example, if you taught evaluation of sources, students can be required to do an annotated bibliography in which they list the criteria that made each source authoritative and valuable for their research.

Some of the skills and processes taught can only be assessed formatively during the inquiry investigation, because they will not be obvious in the final product. One of the most effective means of formative assessment is to provide a graphic organizer that students use to capture the information they discover as they use the skills they have learned. Students could, for example, be asked to take double-column notes from two different perspectives if you taught them to find and evaluate multiple perspectives. You could assess their ability to delineate clearly between the two points of view by looking at their notes. More important, you could identify those students who were having trouble immediately, before they got too far behind and lost the opportunity to take the notes they would need to create an effective final product. If you would like to see examples of formative-assessment graphic organizers on benchmark inquiry skills, you may go to the *New York City Information Fluency Continuum 2010 Priority Benchmark Skills and Assessments* at http://schools.nyc.gov/Academics/LibraryServices/StandardsandCurriculum/.

One caution about assessment to keep in mind is that assessment must always match the type and level of what you have taught. That seems obvious, but we have seen many examples of instructors who require students to display a different level or type of thinking on an assessment product than was taught to them. For example, describing the concept *Dewey Decimal System* as a system of classifying a library collection and then testing them on the memory of the 10 main Dewey classes (e.g., 200s = religion) will result in a mismatch of what is taught and what is assessed.

Case Study #4: Sally and Harry Plan Content

Harry stayed after school to plan his lesson for the next day. He knew that Sally would be assigning her students their research project assignment and then bringing them to the library so that Harry could introduce his instruction on the research process. Sally decided to give students the freedom to choose their own research topics (related to the unit she was teaching), so Harry decides to explore with students what interests them and what they would like to know more about in his first lesson, "How to Choose Just the Right Research Topic." However, the learning audience analysis revealed that some of the students had learned this twenty-first-century learning skill in elementary school and some had not.

Note: Remember to visit our companion website (http://teachingforinquiry.net) for some additional decisions Harry and Sally had to make regarding the content each would cover separately and together.

Extension Questions

1. In his lesson, how might Harry differentiate instruction for those who had already learned this skill and those who were learning it for the first time? Which inquiry skills should be addressed? Which core and clarifying information elements do you think might be most appropriate for Harry's lesson?

2. How will Harry ensure that the students who have already learned how to choose and narrow their research topic aren't bored by his lesson? What enriching elements and ARCS strategies might Harry include in his lesson in order to make sure all students are motivated by his lesson?

References

Ausubel, David. 1978. "In Defense of Advance Organizers: A Reply to the Critics." *Review of Educational Research* 48, no. 2 (Spring): 251–257.

Burgstahler, Sheryl. 2008. "Universal Design of Instruction: From Principles to Practice." In *Universal Design in Higher Education: From Principles to Practice*, edited by Sheryl Burgstahler and Rebecca Cory, 23–44. Boston: Harvard Education Press.

Center for Applied Special Technology (CAST). 2011. "Home: Transforming Education through Universal Design for Learning." Accessed June 3. http://cast.org.

Finn, Chester E. Jr. 1987. *What Works: Research About Teaching and Learning.* Washington, DC: U.S. Department of Education.

Joyce, B. R., and M. Weil. 2000. "Models of Teaching and Learning: Where Do They Come From and How Are They Used?" In *Models of Teaching*, 6th ed., 13–28. Boston: Allyn and Bacon.

Lorayne, Harry, and Jerry Lucas. 1974. *The Memory Book: The Classic Guide to Improving Your Memory at Work, at School, and at Play.* New York: Scarborough House.

New York School Library System. 2010. *Information Fluency Continuum.* New York City Department of Education. http://schools.nyc.gov/Academics/LibraryServices/StandardsandCurriculum/.

Parker, Katie. 2007. "Meeting the Learning and Information Needs of All Students: Universal Design for School Libraries." *Educators' Spotlight Digest* 2, no. 3 (Fall). http://www.informationliteracy.org/users_data/admin/Volume2Issue3_Guest_UniversalDesign_Parker.pdf

Rose, David H., and Anne Meyer. 2002. *Teaching Every Student in the Digital Age: Universal Design for Learning.* Alexandria, VA: ASCD.

Small, Ruth V., and Marilyn P. Arnone. 2002. *Make a PACT for Success: Designing Effective Information Presentations.* Lanham, MD: Scarecrow Press.

Small, R.V., J. Snyder, and K. Parker. 2009. "The Impact of New York's School Libraries on Student Achievement and Motivation: Phase I." *School Library Media Research*, 12. American Library Association. http://www.ala.org/ala/mgrps/divs/aasl/aaslpubsandjournals/slmrb/slmrcontents/volume12/small.cfm.

Stripling, Barbara K., and Judy M. Pitts. 1988. *Brainstorms and Blueprints: Teaching Library Research as a Thinking Process.* Englewood, CO: Libraries Unlimited.

Taylor, Robert S. 1986. *Value Added Processes in Information Systems.* Norwood, NJ: Ablex Publishing.

Tosti, Donald T. 2011. "Feedback and Performance." International Society for Performance Improvement. Accessed September 6. http://www.ispi.org/archives/resources/FeedbackandPerformance_Tosti.pdf.

DIGGING DEEPER

Blue, Elfreda V., and Darra Pace. 2011. "UD and UDL: Paving the Way Toward Inclusion and Independence in the School Library." *Knowledge Quest* 39, no. 3 (January/February): 48–57.

Copeland, Clayton A. 2011. "School Librarians of the 21st Century: Using Resources and Assistive Technologies to Support Students' Differences and Abilities." *Knowledge Quest* 39, no. 3 (January/February): 64–69.

Franklin, Renee E. 2011. "Before the Bell Rings: The Importance of Preparing Pre-service School Librarians to Serve Students with Special Needs." *Knowledge Quest* 39, no. 3 (January/February): 58–63.

Hancock, Vicki E. 1993. "Information Literacy for Lifelong Learning." ERIC Digest, ERIC Clearinghouse on Information Resources, Syracuse, NY. ED358870.

Kuhlthau, Carol C. 1989. "Information Search Process: A Summary of Research and Implications for School Library Media Programs." *School Library Media Quarterly* 18 (Fall): 19–25.

Plotnick, Eric. 1997. "Concept Mapping: A Graphical System for Understanding the Relationship between Concepts." ERIC Digest, ERIC Clearinghouse on Information and Technology, Syracuse, NY. ED407938.

Tomlinson, Carol A. 2000. "Reconcilable Differences? Standards-Based Teaching and Differentiation." *Educational Leadership* 58 , no. 1 (September): 6–11.

Technique for Inquiry Teaching and Learning

Mr. Smith's fifth graders had been studying animal adaptation for the past few days. They had read from their textbooks, answered the questions at the end of the chapter, and watched a short video. Today they were going online to search the Internet to find facts on their topics. As they were culling through Google, Marc asked his classmate at the next computer, "What are we looking for again?"

Introduction

How we teach is as important as what we teach. Mr. Smith presented background information and used technology in his lesson but he didn't use instructional methods that engaged students in their learning. They collected facts, and learning facts alone does not enable students to acquire the abilities and understanding they will need for the twenty-first century. Learning begins with student engagement. "Engaged students are trying to make meaning of what they are learning" (Barkley, 2009) and Marc obviously was not engaged in animal adaptation; he was going through the motions.

In Chapter 1 we discussed that the transformation of information to knowledge and knowledge to understanding does not happen without the intervention of good teaching. Through the processes of application and constructive thinking, learners convert information and knowledge to understanding. Both inquiry and motivation are essential components of instruction that push students to reach for deep understanding. Student engagement is the product of motivation and active learning as inquiry frames the process. Thoughtfully choosing instructional methods is essential to help students make sense of what they are learning and to become engaged in their learning. Before deciding which technique(s) you will use, it is helpful to think back to your purpose (e.g., Are there any existing barriers that may prohibit the use of some media?), your audience (e.g., Do you have a range of student learning styles that require a variety of teaching methods?), and your content (e.g., Is some of your content best presented through demonstrations and hands-on practice?). As you begin to determine and develop your teaching techniques for your lesson, be sure to situate them in a constructivist context in which teaching strategies are tailored to student needs.

There are several dimensions to a constructivist context in which teaching technique is tailored to student needs, including the following:

- Differentiating instruction
- Inquiry and standards
- Instructional methods
- Learning support materials
- Web 2.0 technology
- Evaluation

Each of these factors is addressed in the following sections of this chapter. Each section addresses the importance of inquiry, motivation, and active learning in delivering effective instruction.

Essential Questions

- How do we best teach what the students need to know and be able to do? How do we use technology to support the inquiry process?
- How do we know that students learned what we taught?

Chapter Outcomes and Indicators

By the end of this chapter and by taking advantage of this book's companion website (http://teachingforinquiry.net), you will be able to achieve the following learning outcomes and indicators:

1. OUTCOME: Recognize that teaching for understanding is a result of the combination of inquiry and motivation and is achieved through differentiation of instruction in the library.
   a. INDICATOR: Understand how to differentiate through resources, inquiry questions based on student interests, and teaching and learning strategies.
   b. INDICATOR: Understand teaching strategies that engage students in active inquiry that is aligned with their individual needs and interests.
2. OUTCOME: Understand the different instructional methods to effectively engage students to learn skills, concepts, and content.
   a. INDICATOR: Identify and describe at least three teaching strategies.
   b. INDICATOR: Explain why one strategy is better suited to a particular learning context than another.
3. OUTCOME: Understand how technology supports student motivation and the inquiry learning process.
   a. INDICATOR: Identify at least three types of Web 2.0 tools/services that can be used to support each phase of the inquiry learning process.
   b. INDICATOR: Align three different types of Web 2.0 tools to key indicators from AASL's *Standards for the 21st-Century Learner.*
4. OUTCOME: Understand how to evaluate your teaching strategies.
   a. INDICATOR: Write three outcomes-based evaluation statements.
   b. INDICATOR: Develop three strategies to improve instruction based on evaluation results.
   c. INDICATOR: Recognize the impact of the digital environment on inquiry.

Differentiating Instruction in the Library

The concept of differentiation has been misunderstood and misapplied by educators who struggle to accommodate a wide range of student abilities and interests. Differentiation does not mean holding different (lower) expectations for the content learning or level of thought for struggling students. It does mean offering extra support and a variety of approaches to learning, so that all students have the opportunity to master the content and skills.

Differentiation through Resources

Librarians are in a prime position to offer differentiated learning experiences through ready access to resources in a variety of formats and languages. You can ensure that the resources offer the same level of content, but some information is presented graphically, some through video or audio, some through text.

Differentiation through Inquiry Questions Based on Student Interest

Resources are only part of the differentiation process for content learning, however. Library investigations can be designed to allow students to pursue individual questions and topics while focusing on the same larger idea or essential question. For example, Marc's class research assignment could have revolved around the essential questions: How can animals adapt to their environment to increase their chances of survival? What are some physical or behavioral adaptations the animals demonstrate? You, as the librarian, can help students narrow their investigations to aspects of the essential questions while still enabling them to choose a topic that personally interests them (e.g., How are oil spills in the ocean harmful to ocean life and humans?).

Differentiation through Instruction Targeted to Student Needs

Helping students select individual topics/questions that fulfill their personal interests and connect to the unit concept/essential questions is the easier part of differentiating instruction for librarians. Effective differentiation also involves teaching students to be active learners who use a variety of learning strategies/skills and designing instruction so that students have opportunities to practice and repeat the strategies and skills until they achieve understanding. Those strategies and skills form the basis of teaching for understanding in the library.

Determining the strategies and skills that individual students need to learn is a daunting task for librarians because you are not with the same students every day, nor do you have a lot of time with them in the library to assess their level of skill development before they have to start using the skills to pursue their investigations. You may use one of the following strategies to make sure that you and the students are targeting the skills that they need before pursuing a specific inquiry investigation:

- *Scaffolding:* Isolate the one or two skills that you plan to teach and scaffold the other necessary skills. For example, if you plan to teach evaluation of websites, then you might prepare a webliography of appropriate sites to scaffold the search strategy process. Students can then focus on evaluating the sites you have selected.

- *Diagnostic Test:* You may prepare a simple diagnostic test that asks students to answer questions about the relevant inquiry skills or name the steps in performing a task. For example, you could give students statements pulled from a general periodical article about the topic and ask them to quickly identify those that are fact and those that are opinion. A quick check of students' performance will reveal those who need instruction on fact vs. opinion.

- *Diagnostic Task:* You might give students a simple task to perform that will illustrate their skill level. For example, if you want to determine if students know how to pick the most appropriate books for their topics/questions, you might do a modified scavenger hunt by giving students individual topics and Dewey ranges and asking them to find the "best" book and bring it back to their seat. On their "quick write" sheets, students will list their reasons for selecting that book. Students who do not know to check the navigational aids of a book to find the best match to research questions are those who need additional instruction.

- *Self-Reflection:* Students can be taught to reflect on their own skill levels. You can provide reflective questions or a rubric to help them assess their own needs for instruction.

- *Mini-lesson with Guided Practice:* If you are not sure about the students' ability to perform the necessary skills, you can deliver a mini-lesson with modeling and guided practice. This lesson will serve as a quick review for those who have developed the skills and as an awareness session for others who have not mastered the skill. The guided practice segment will allow you and the students themselves to decide who would benefit from additional instruction.

Instructional Methods

Instructional methods are ways that are used to teach students concepts, content, and skills. They tend to fall into two categories: teacher-centered approaches and student-centered approaches. You can use many methods to engage learners in the content of your lesson. While several of them are discussed here, this is neither meant to be an exhaustive list nor imply that methods cannot be combined. In fact, in most cases you will want to use two or more of these methods to make your lesson more interesting and participative. The best approach is learner-centered, inquiry-based, technology-rich curricula. Learner-centered approaches, often referred to as active or discovery learning, are grounded in constructivism and involve instruction where the teacher is a facilitator or guide as the learners construct their own understandings. They typically:

- reflect the notion of the learner as the primary focus,
- emphasize the importance of participatory learning,
- incorporate hands-on learning or working in groups, and
- include inquiry and student-driven questions and reflection.

As you read about the following methods, keep in mind your goals and objectives, the needs and characteristics of your learning audience, and the content you wish to present:

- Questioning
- Practice
- Discussion
- Brainstorming
- Role-playing
- Gaming
- Lecture

Questioning

Questioning is a technique used to generate high-level inquiry and thinking that may be used with other techniques, such as lectures and discussions. It is an ideal technique for a constructivist-learning environment focused on solving one or more relevant issues or problems. Questions can flow in three possible ways—from student to teacher, teacher to student, and from student to student. Using questions can:

- provide interactivity and increase student participation,
- identify student misperceptions,
- allow feedback, and
- stimulate reflective thinking.

Effective questioning is both an art and a science. Here are some rules of thumb.

Vary the cognitive level of your questions. Occasionally, you will want to ask lower-level questions that demonstrate remembering and comprehending, particularly when new content is first introduced, in order to stimulate student participation and make sure that students have a clear understanding of the content taught. Even under those circumstances, you should move quickly to questions that stimulate and develop students' higher-order, reflective, and critical-thinking skills through application, analysis, evaluation, and creation.

Avoid certain kinds of questions. For example, asking a question that requires a yes-or-no response provides no information about a student's learning. You can either follow up a yes/no question with a question probe that asks for further explanation and information or simply ask a higher-order question initially.

Avoid asking questions that result in useless responses (e.g., "Does everyone understand how to use the inquiry model?"); questions that inhibit responses (e.g., "I've explained how to do a research paper twice now. Does anyone *still* have any questions?"); and questions that are unclear or too broad (e.g., What do you know about inquiry skills?"). The first type of question, when answered, does not provide enough specific information to be helpful. Try focusing on one skill or one stage of the inquiry process. The second type acts as a put-down and discourages response. After all, who wants to look incompetent in front of peers? The final question type is too vague to be answered.

Sometimes you may find yourself asking complex questions—those that have several parts or require more than one answer. If possible, try to restate complex questions, breaking them down when necessary. This will help to eliminate confusion and build students' learning confidence.

Call on different individuals to avoid the same students answering all the time. There are many different perspectives on this issue. Some believe in calling on students to answer questions even if they haven't raised their hands and even if it embarrasses them when they cannot answer. Others prefer to call on only those with hands raised, even though some students are likely never to have an opportunity to respond. One strategy to alleviate the pressure that some students feel when called upon to respond is to ask them to think about it and you'll come back to them later. Usually they'll have thought of a response by the time you return to them. Another solution to this dilemma is to provide in advance at least some of the questions you plan to ask students. Then they will have an opportunity to prepare their answers, and everyone should be able to respond successfully.

Give students adequate time to respond. Have you ever thought about how much time you give students to respond when you ask a question? Mary Budd Rowe (e.g., 1987, 1996) has. She conducted research to see exactly how much time, on average, teachers waited after asking a question before they blurted out the answer. What do you think she found—20 seconds? 10 seconds? 5 seconds?

Rowe's findings suggest that we are uncomfortable with the periods of silence that occur between our questions and students' responses. The average wait time was 0.9 seconds, and the greatest amount of wait time was about 1.5 seconds in typical classrooms. Think about it: when you ask students a question, you know the answer because you have been thinking about it in preparation for the lesson and you know more about the topic than your students. But your students need time to retrieve an answer from their long-term memories. Even a computer often takes more than 0.9 seconds to retrieve information.

In later studies, researchers discovered that if we allow students three to five seconds to respond to our questions after asking them, we'll not only get *more* answers but we'll also get *better answers* (Casteel and Stahl, 1973; Rowe, 1987; Tobin, 1987). Not only that, but they found that teachers' questioning strategies improved; they asked a greater variety of questions, increased the quality of their questions (and decreased the quantity), and asked questions requiring higher-level thinking by students.

> **TIME OUT!**
>
> When you ask students a question, you know the answer because you have been thinking about it in preparation for the lesson and you know more about the topic than your students. But your students must retrieve an answer from their long-term memory. Even a computer often takes more than 0.9 seconds to retrieve information.

While 3 to 5 seconds may seem very short, take out a watch with a second hand and wait 5 seconds. In front of a class, that can seem like a long time to you and your students. So, prepare them ahead of time for the wait. Tell them about Dr. Rowe's study and how you are going to give them 5 seconds to respond each time you ask a question. They'll likely find this idea fascinating and won't be surprised with the silence after your question.

The next time you are in front of a group and ask a question, count to 5 in your mind. You may be surprised with the results (and you may find that students pay more attention to your questions).

Reinforce responses. When students offer responses to your question, you can reinforce these positive behaviors and encourage more of them. One strategy is to build on key points students make. This increases students' confidence and encourages additional discussion. Another strategy is to ask the student to restate the response in a different way (you may need to help) so that everyone is sure to understand it. Finally, informative feedback that is objective and nonjudgmental allows students to know about their learning progress and achievement.

Don't be afraid to admit you don't know. You are not expected to know everything about everything. When you don't know something, tell students. Turn it into a learning experience and search for the answer together. This can be a very satisfying experience for you and for your students.

Even though questioning is an effective technique for stimulating student participation and interactivity, be careful not to overuse it. In a study to determine the types of motivational strategies library media specialists use in their instruction, Small (1999) found that there were three instructional situations in which student motivation appeared to decrease: (1) physically moving students from one instructional location to another (e.g., moving from the library to the computer lab); (2) using a technique inappropriately (e.g., asking off-track questions like, "How was your trip to California?); and (3) overusing a technique (specifically, asking too many questions in a single lesson). Students became bored with questions quickly, the questions no longer were motivating, and students began to exhibit off-task behaviors.

Practice

Providing opportunities for students to practice their knowledge and skills is an essential part of the learning process. Research indicates that learning is more effective when students are given varied practice experiences (Levin and Long, 1981). As discussed in Chapter 4, an effective method to teach a skill is to structure a lesson around four phases:

- Direct instruction and demonstration of the skill
- Guided practice
- Independent practice
- Reflection

Practice activities might occur following instruction or can be used as an exercise during your lesson. They can incorporate any of the support materials previously described. Practice allows you to provide feedback to students on their knowledge or skill development *before* they have to apply it to their assignments or projects.

Here are some examples of practice activities during or following a lesson that you may want to try.

- After demonstrating a specific database, students practice locating materials on a variety of given topics within the database.
- After a lesson on web-evaluation skills, students are asked to evaluate a few specific websites using the instrument demonstrated during the instruction.
- After being introduced to the Dewey Decimal System, students are given a range of Dewey Decimal numbers and must identify the subject area for each number.

Discussion Strategies

Discussion is an interactive, motivating instructional technique. It allows you to share control of the lessons with your students.

- Using discussion will increase learning retention and provide more opportunity for student engagement.
- Discussions allow students a chance to test their hypotheses and challenge others' ideas.
- Discussions provide opportunities for interaction and application of content learned through other media and methods.
- Discussions often stimulate a desire for continued learning.
- Through discussions, teachers can make some assessment about learning and provide feedback.
- Discussions can easily be integrated into most lessons.

While discussion is a powerful content-delivery method, some teachers resist using it because it can be time consuming, they are fearful that the class will get "off-track," and they worry that important content will not be covered. To avoid these problems, you need to prepare students fully for a discussion. Perhaps there is something you can give them to read first, or you might provide them with a question set (advance organizer) to ponder in advance. This is a particularly effective motivator for students who seldom voluntarily participate because it allows them to think through their responses before having to share them with the larger group.

Provide ground rules for discussions (e.g., intended goal, amount of time, participation requirements). This will help alleviate some of the fears about including discussions in your lesson. Consider setting up some general rules for each discussion and establish them with each lesson.

Keeping in mind that constructivist learning environments allow students enough time for thinking and discovering, be flexible in extending the allotted time, if possible, when a discussion has engendered a great deal of excitement and participation. It is also essential to establish an environment of trust so that all students feel comfortable in participating in the discussion.

How do you get a discussion going? There are many ways. You can use a discussion "trigger," such as a question or problem to solve. You might use 5–10-minute videos to stimulate thinking and discussion on a specific topic. Other common prompts, such as role-play or demonstration, a controversial statement, a thought-provoking question, or a brief anecdote, are also effective as triggers. Discussion triggers are a great motivational strategy for gaining students' attention.

As the discussion gets going, remember that in constructivist-learning environments, your role is that of a facilitator, not a discussion leader, so step back from it somewhat. Try to remain neutral, keeping the discussion moving forward and on track but not dominating. Offering occasional feedback on especially important points may be appropriate.

As with all effectively implemented presentation methods, prepare students in advance for the activity. You'll also need to "prepare" your learning space. If possible, arrange seats in a circle or rectangle so that all students are face-to-face and therefore more likely to participate. If your discussion is extensive or covers several topics, periodically provide a summary of key points or, with older students, appoint someone to provide the summaries. At the end of any discussion, it is essential that an overall summary be provided.

Two types of Web 2.0 social networking tools (Ning and Edmodo) and content collaboration tools (Wikispaces and Edublogs) enable online discussion. Educators can use "blended" learning to introduce these tools to the students in class and have them interact in the discussion after school or in the evening. Students enjoy using emerging technologies in their learning as a "natural extension of the way they are currently living and learning outside the classroom" (Project Tomorrow, 2010: 3).

Brainstorming

Most likely, at some point in your life you have participated in a brainstorming session either at work or in school. Brainstorming is a simple, easy-to-use, and very effective technique for facilitating creative thinking and problem solving and for encouraging student participation. Brainstorming is a highly motivational activity because (1) it is fun, so it gains and maintains students' attention and (2) all ideas are welcome and (if properly executed) never criticized, thereby helping to build students' confidence.

This technique can be used with any age group. It is almost always used in conjunction with another (follow-up) activity, for example, as a basis for discussion or to initiate selection of a research topic. Most brainstorming activities are conducted with groups of 5–15 persons but it has been done successfully with as many as 200 people. Large groups can be broken into smaller ones for a brainstorming exercise.

Brainstorming should be conducted in an informal, relaxed atmosphere. Before beginning, make sure that you have a method for recording responses that everyone can see, such as a blackboard or whiteboard or, with larger groups, projection using a computer-based system or an overhead projector. You can record the responses or, better yet, choose a student to act as recorder (this would be especially motivating for a student who is high in need for power). Web 2.0 tools that support brainstorming are Edistorm (http://edistorm.com) and Mindmeister (http://www.meindmeister.com). For brainstorming rules, see Figure 5.1.

Figure 5.1. Rules for Brainstorming

1. Review the rules for brainstorming with your students.
   - All ideas should be acknowledged.
   - No criticism should be made of any suggestions, no matter how radical.
   - Wherever possible, build on others' ideas.
   - Think creatively and intelligently.
2. To conduct a successful brainstorming session, briefly state the problem, question, or issue. This can come from you or the students.
3. Stress that all ideas are welcome and that quantity is more important than quality at this point in the activity.
4. Participants take turns offering ideas. When waiting for their turn, students should be encouraged to write their own ideas on a piece of paper to avoid forgetting them in the excitement of the activity.
5. Once all ideas are offered, review them with students and ask them to choose the best one(s) for solving the problem, answering the question, or resolving the issue.

Brainstorming is a particularly useful technique for inquiry skills instruction. It can be used to suggest topics for research papers, identify the range of resources that can be used for gathering information for a research project (e.g., human, print, mediated), or determine different ways students can present the results of their research projects (e.g., a paper, a model, a computer-based presentation).

An alternative to brainstorming is brainwriting (Van Gundy, 1988). In brainwriting, students individually write down all of their ideas on a piece of paper and then exchange their papers with other students, who then modify or make suggestions about those ideas in writing. Once this is done, it would be useful for students to share their ideas with the entire group.

Role-Playing

Role-playing is a method of instruction that involves the spontaneous, unprepared dramatization or acting out of a realistic situation by two or more individuals under an instructor's guidance. Players are presented with a problem situation (real or fictional) from which their dialogue develops. Enactment is followed by debriefing and discussion. It's a meaningful, creative, and highly motivating educational activity, particularly in the area of inquiry instruction. See Figure 5.2 for some tips for effective role-playing.

In instructional settings, role-playing can be used as a follow-up to a lecture or some other instructional presentation (e.g., video) from which a problem situation is derived. It is an effective method

> **STOP! THINK! DO!**
>
> Can you think of one or more information problem-based situations that would make an excellent role-play exercise?

for helping students to understand the feelings and perspectives of others when faced with a problem or conflict situation. Participants often discover or develop new ways to handle problem situations. It is also an excellent vehicle for promoting reflective thinking about a problem, various alternative solutions, and how those solutions might affect others. See Figure 5.3 for detailed steps on how to conduct a role-play.

The discussion is an essential part of the role-play. This is where the roles are revealed and the major part of the learning takes place. It allows the group to discover important rules and ideas from the experience. Following this initial discussion, there is an opportunity to reenact

---

Figure 5.2. Tips for Effective Role-Playing

- Role-playing must be carried out in a learning environment where even the shyest students feel safe to try out new ideas and behaviors.
- Make sure your role-play has a clear and useful purpose. Tie it to a research project or one of the students' information problems to ensure relevance.
- Keep the role-play situation as simple and brief as possible, yet challenging and nonthreatening to motivate active participation.
- Assign certain members of the group their roles (carefully select your players so that students are not placed in a role they find personally offensive or intimidating) while assigning all others as observers. It is essential that all participants have a role, either as players or observers. This will help to sustain the attention of all your students throughout this activity.
- Players should be given some time to prepare their roles in private. This will help build confidence in their ability to effectively play the assigned role. Players *should not* discuss their roles with each other.
- Once players leave the room to prepare their roles, observers should be assigned either one or more players to observe or particular phenomena to observe across players (e.g., body language, tone of voice, style). This ensures that all observers will be as involved in the activity as the players. Total participation helps to make the role-play a satisfying learning experience for all students.
- Your "role" is to provide just enough time for the role-playing activity and make sure the role-play does not go too far or get too personal. This is helpful for maintaining students' confidence in a safe and trusting learning environment.

Source: Adapted from Wright, 1989.

---

the role-play using different players, if desired. The reenactment may have different goals than the initial role-play.

Gaming

Games have been used as instructional presentation methods for many years. These range from simple word games to spelling and geography bees, from challenging mathematical brain teasers to complex computer simulations. Games will enrich your core information and provide opportunities for the students to apply what they are learning in a structured learning environment. You can use games to review content that has already been taught, to introduce new content, or to apply learned content to new situations. Motivationally, games provide the types of competitive activities on which students with high need for power thrive.

Games can be instructor developed, student developed, or a combination. For example, you could develop a basic game and then have students develop rules and provide more details. In this way, the game itself, in addition to the content of the game, becomes part of the learning experience and more relevant to students. Games can also be used as periodic learning checks.

In a 2008 research study from the Pew Internet and American Life Project, "Teens, Video Games and Civics," it was found that "Video gaming is pervasive in the lives of American teens—young teens and older teens, girls and boys, and teens from across the socioeconomic spectrum. Opportunities for gaming are everywhere, and teens are playing video games frequently" (Lenhart et al., 2008). Using gaming in educational settings opens the doors for new possibilities in teaching and learning. "Children develop skills that connect and manipulate information in the virtual world of video games without really knowing that they're learning. Rather than fight what children obviously enjoy and what is natural for them, the enticement of games can be

Figure 5.3. Conducting a Role-Play

Phase One: Warming Up the Group
- Identify or introduce the problem.
- Briefly discuss the problem.
- Explain the rules of the role-playing activity.

Phase Two: Selecting Role Players
- Select the role players carefully.

Phase Three: Setting the Stage
- Provide all students with the same problem scenario.
- Provide each player with a description of his or her role.
- Instruct players not to discuss their roles with each other.

Phase Four: Preparing the Observers
- Provide observers with clear directions on their tasks. For example, you might want to assign some to observe one player and others to observe others, telling all of them what to look for and record.

Phase Five: Enactment
- Conduct the role-play.
- Stop the role-play at the appropriate time (when it begins to be redundant or players run out of ideas).
- Assemble all participants for debriefing and discussion.

Phase Six: Discussion
- Review/summarize the enactment.
- Role-players reveal their roles.
- Observers share their perceptions.
- Prepare for a reenactment.

Phase Seven: Reenactment
- Repeat the role-play with different actors. This step is often omitted.

Phase Eight: Discussion/Evaluation
- Review/summarize the reenactment.
- Observers share their perceptions.
- Discuss differences in results and perceptions.

Phase Nine: Sharing and Generalizing
- Discuss how the role-play applies to students' own situations.
- Generalize to other situations.

Source: Adapted from Shaftel and Shaftel, 1967.

used to enhance K–12 education" (Annetta, 2007). Games, if done right, can become a powerful tool to get groups to work together. According to Elliott Masie (2011), gaming allows learners to "fail to success." This concept of failing forward allows learners to test their limits in a safe environment. In addition, gaming increases muscle memory, or the rehearsal necessary to solidify correct behavior. Finally, gaming increases an internal and external competitive spirit related to learning opportunities. An educational game, one designed for learning, is a subset of both play and fun. It is a melding of educational content, learning principles, and computer games (Prensky, 2001). Digital game-based learning is organized to provide both education and pleasure. Play relaxes people, putting them in a receptive state for learning.

The Flow of Gaming

Anyone who has visited a video-game arcade or watched a child using Nintendo or Game Boy knows how motivating games and simulations are for young people. Children often spend hours at them seeming to be almost hypnotized by the activity. This state, in which attention is intensely focused on a specific activity and players become so completely immersed in that activity that they lose track of time or space, is referred to as *flow* (Csikszentmihalyi, 1990).

Flow epitomizes a state of heightened curiosity and intrinsic motivation. You have probably experienced flow at one time or another, perhaps when completing a challenging jigsaw puzzle, playing solitaire, reading a book, or creating a display.

While it is easy to see how a person can get into flow when playing a game or when involved in a simulation experience, it is important to know that flow can occur during almost any type of activity. Csikszentmihalyi (1990) discovered that the phenomenon existed when people were performing such different activities as playing chess, ballet dancing, and doing construction work, as long as the activity included these four main elements: an appropriate level of challenge, curiosity stimulation, clearly defined goals, and immediate and useful feedback on progress toward a goal.

Csikszentmihalyi (1990) discovered that for flow to occur, there must be a balance between challenge and skill. If people participate in an activity in which the challenges are greater than their skills, they will feel anxious and frustrated. If people's skills are greater than challenges, they feel boredom. If balanced, people will get involved in an activity, and that activity has high potential for flow and enjoyment.

You feel fortunate when your students enter a state of flow during one of your lessons. Research has found a positive relationship between flow and exploratory behavior, which forms the foundation of inquiry. A personal example from one of the authors will illustrate the power of flow:

> *One morning several years ago, when I was an elementary school librarian, I was working with a group of 12 sixth grade students on a unit of censorship. I had put a group of books, all which had been banned at some time or other (e.g.,* The Diary of Anne Frank, The Five Chinese Brothers, Webster's Dictionary*), on a cart in front of them. I explained to the students what was meant by censorship, describing some instances of censorship in their lives (as when their parents wouldn't allow them to watch certain television shows or see certain movies), had them brainstorm other examples, and then showed them the cart of banned books. Their job was to read the books and determine why they thought they have been considered offensive by someone.*
>
> *One of the students in the group, Mark, although very bright, was not a highly motivated student. According to his classroom teacher, he had a short attention span and sometimes had difficulty focusing on a learning task. He liked to have fun and was a bit of a class clown.*
>
> *The students set to work on the books and I, too, was caught up in the activity, reading alongside the students. All of a sudden, Mark looked up and exclaimed, "Holy cow—it's one o'clock! We missed lunch!!" Of course we were all startled and the students couldn't understand where the time had gone. We were so engrossed in the activity, we totally lost track of time. We had all entered a state of flow!*

Usually, flow occurs when you are actively involved in a difficult task that stretches your capabilities and challenges you. You become totally absorbed and focused on achieving a clearly defined goal. As you continue working, you get immediate feedback about how well you are proceeding toward that goal. You gain a sense of control over the activity and soon you are so intensely focused that you block out all other thoughts and distractions and become lost in the activity. This type of experience can be extremely satisfying for the learner.

Games and simulations are experiences with high flow potential. With technology, we are now able to deliver very sophisticated learning games and simulations even to our youngest learners. Simulations, like brainstorming and role-playing, are a constructivist tool for problem-based learning. Brainstorming, role-playing, games, and simulations are presentation methods that are particularly appealing to students who have a high need for affiliation and a high need for power because they require group interaction and offer an opportunity for students to exert leadership or to try to influence others about their point of view or ideas on a topic. If you have ever watched children surf the web, play a video game, or watch an exciting video, you can appreciate the high-flow potential of experiences that incorporate media or technology.

Lecture

Lecture is one of the most common forms of instructional presentation techniques, even with very young students. Yet, research indicates that only 5 percent of material a student learns through lecture is retained over time. When instruction becomes interactive and students are given opportunities to actively participate and apply what they have learned, that retention rate climbs to 95 percent.

Researchers at Mid-Continent Research for Education and Learning (McREL) have identified instructional strategies that are most likely to improve achievement across all content areas and across all grade levels (Marzano, Pickering, and Pollock, 2001). These strategies can be incorporated into the lecture to increase student involvement and motivation. Several are listed here with suggested Web 2.0 applications that can be integrated for increased motivation and engagement (see the later section "A Sampling of Web 2.0 Tools," pp. 112–117, for descriptions of these resources):

Identifying Similarities and Differences
- Mindmeister, http://www.mindmeister.com
- Spicynodes, http://www.spicynodes.com

Summarizing and Note Taking
- Evernote, http://www.evernote.com
- Livebinders, http://livebinders.com

Nonlinguistic Representations
- Wordle, http://www.wordle.net
- Prezi, http://www.prezi.com

Questions and Advance Organizers
- Animoto, http://animoto.com
- Polleverywhere, http://polleverywhere.com

While facts and opinions can only be stated as is, there are many ways to present concepts, principles, and procedures to make them more interesting and interactive. In a study on student interest and boredom, Small, Dodge, and Jiang (1996) found that *colorful* instruction, instruction that incorporates a variety of attention-gaining and maintaining strategies, appears to be the most effective for generating interest and preventing boredom. Divide and present information about the concept, principle, or procedure in small, logical chunks and provide examples or analogies for each chunk. If possible, find ways to add to each chunk some enriching information, such as questions (with feedback), student-created examples, analogies, or personal anecdotes. For example, introduce your lecture with an interesting story of a time when you were faced with a difficult information problem: present an overview of your chosen inquiry model; go back and talk about each part of the model, giving examples and asking your audience to provide their own examples of each part. Conclude your lecture with the rest of your story, describing how you used your inquiry model to solve that information problem. And don't forget that *you* are part of the message. Your body language can contribute to making your lecture boring.

You can motivate your learning audience through such techniques, as well as with voice level and inflection, pacing, eye contact, and enthusiasm. Also, have you ever noticed that when you have to teach the same lesson more than once it seems to improve with each successive presentation? That's because each lesson serves as practice for the subsequent one. As you find that practice improves your presentation over time, you will discover yourself adding new enriching elements or motivational strategies, partly to keep yourself motivated and challenged.

Learning-Support Materials and Activities

A number of relevant support materials and activities can be used within or following a lesson to reinforce the information taught. Some examples of useful support materials are handouts, learning centers, and job aids. Handouts are generally provided during a lesson while job aids are typically provided after the lesson has been taught. Learning centers are often used in place of a lesson.

Handouts

> **WORDS OF WISDOM**
>
> When developing handouts, make sure of the following:
>
> - They are error-free.
> - You have enough copies for everyone.
> - They look good (e.g., some interesting graphics, lots of white space, well-organized).
> - You have made them available online with appropriate links to additional relevant information.

Handouts are generally intended to reinforce or enhance your lesson content. Some handouts may allow students to practice a skill that was taught or include details you don't have time to present in your lesson. People love to walk away from an instructional presentation with something tangible. A handout provides students with information they can use to introduce or follow along during the lesson or it can offer review or enrichment information for referral after the lesson is over. A wiki (http://www.wikispaces.com) can be effectively used to post handouts and other materials from a presentation or workshop; participants can access the information online after the session. In addition, the presenter can easily and quickly post extra information in response to questions or comments during the session. If you decide to give students your handout during the lesson, be sure it includes an outline of key points only. Too much text often results in students' focusing on reading the handout rather than paying attention to the lesson.

Learning Centers

Learning centers are self-contained modules of individualized, self-paced materials that students may work through independently. They are sometimes called learning stations or interest centers. Learning centers:

- Focus on a particular topic or subject area. They may be used as a tutorial to assist students in knowledge or skill development, to help develop learning confidence, or as enrichment for reinforcing the student's motivation to go beyond what they have already learned.

- Incorporate print materials or computer-assisted instruction, audiovisual tools, interactive video, and other resources. They should include detailed, explicit directions for completing all activities in the learning center and some type of assessment method.

- Are most effective when they are structured, active, and appealing. Research centers, literacy centers, writing centers, and listening centers are common types of learning centers in library media centers in school libraries.

Job Aids

Job aids are performance-support tools; they are often used to reinforce instruction. Some examples of job aids are posters (e.g., the choking-victim poster found in many restaurants); online help systems (e.g., an online income-tax-calculation help system); and help sheets (e.g., the handout version of PowerPoint slides from a presentation). Job aids can come in a variety of forms—job-aid mouse pads, job-aid mobiles, job-aid post-its, job aids that frame a computer monitor, job-aid posters, freestanding and cube-shaped job aids.

Job aids are used to help someone perform a repetitive task until it is learned, a complicated task that is infrequently performed, or a task for which the rules or content change frequently by providing a reference to the precise, essential step in that task whenever the need arises (Rossett and Gautier-Downs, 1991). They can be created in print or electronic form. In the school library, job aids can be used to help students perform such tasks as using an online database, finding a book on the shelves, or searching the online catalog.

QR (Quick Response) Codes have recently entered the library/educational arena as digital job aids. A QR Code is a specific matrix barcode (or two-dimensional code), readable by smartphones that have the correct reader application (free). The code consists of black modules arranged in a square pattern on a white background. The information encoded can be text, URL, or other data. Librarians can generate QR codes to have students access websites, videos, text documents, etc., with additional information to support their learning. An example appears in Figure 5.4.

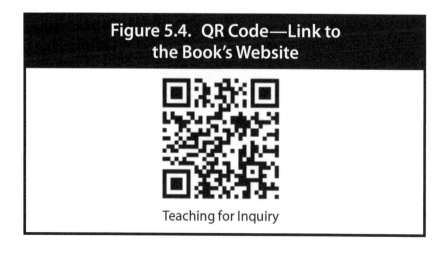

Figure 5.4. QR Code—Link to the Book's Website

Teaching for Inquiry

Angie Tilaro and Allison Rossett (1993), in "Creating Motivating Job Aids," created an excellent chart that describes ways in which Keller's ARCS model can be applied to the design of job aids for adult training. Many of these same strategies are adaptable to job aids for K–12 instruction; for example, (1) replace words with pictures and use color, highlighting, boldface, and bullets (for capturing and maintaining attention); (2) let students participate in job aid creation (to help make the job aid more relevant); (3) teach students to use the job aid (to ensure students' confidence); and (4) recognize successful use of job aids (to promote learning satisfaction).

Teaching Techniques and Learning Styles

The methods described in this chapter are only a few of the many ways you can present content to your students. But how do you know which methods to use with whom and when? Maybe it's time to return once again to the audience analysis.

In Chapter 3, you learned about Kolb's experiential learning model, which identified four stages to the learning cycle: concrete experience, observation and reflection, abstract-concept formation, and new applications. Svinicki and Dixon (1987) identified a number of teaching and learning activities that support each of Kolb's stages. No matter what the grade level, for students at the concrete stage of learning (i.e., a new experience in which content may be difficult or abstract), they recommend such learning activities as labs, observations, hands-on activities, games, and simulations.

> **STOP! THINK! DO!**
>
> What other techniques can be used to make abstract or complex content more concrete?

As students move into the reflective-observation stage, they prefer watching others or reflecting on their own experiences. Bandura's (1982) social learning theory describes the effectiveness of learning from direct experiences, observation, and modeled behavior. Modeled behavior, according to Bandura, can come from real-life observations, such as observing an instructor or another student, or through vicarious observations (e.g., a computer-based simulation, a video). Students at this stage benefit from such activities as keeping journals, discussions, demonstrations (either real life or vicarious), questioning, and brainstorming.

At the active experimentation stage, students begin using what they are learning to solve problems and make decisions. Such activities as case studies, debates (these are particularly appealing to students high in need for power), simulations, fieldwork, internships, and homework assignments are most appropriate for students trying out their new knowledge while in this active experimentation stage. That ancient Chinese proverb comes to mind: "Tell me, I forget. Show me, I remember. Involve me, I understand." The use of interactive techniques, in which students actively participate and apply what they are learning, will result in the highest levels of learning and motivation.

In the abstract-conceptualization stage, learners make hypotheses and create theories to explain what they have observed. At this stage, they need fewer hands-on activities and more "thinking" activities. Svinicki and Dixon (1987) recommend such activities as lectures, model building, analogy development, and research papers and projects for students at this stage of the experimental learning process.

In situations where students are learning something unfamiliar or difficult, any extrinsic rewards valued by the students may be an effective motivator in the short term (particularly with underachievers). Providing encouragement and praise to all students as they make progress toward achieving learning goals is one of the most powerful techniques for fostering continuing motivation. But remember, any reward, to be effective, must be relevant to the learning task and tied to authentic learning effort and achievement. Helping students attribute their learning performance to their own effort and ability will have a direct impact on their ongoing expectations for success.

Evaluation

The purpose of evaluation is to (1) provide accountability, (2) measure the effectiveness (both strengths and weaknesses) of your instruction in accomplishing your goals, and (3) identify opportunities to improve your instructional program. Often, we think of evaluation as happening *after* instruction has ended. One type of evaluation allows you to evaluate your instruction and instructional materials *before* they are delivered to your target learning audience. Some call this type of evaluation *formative* evaluation (because it is conducted while your instruction is still in its formative stage), but it can also be thought of as *informative* evaluation because it informs you so that you can make revisions before actual delivery.

Formative Evaluation

Formative evaluation is an interactive process in which you evaluate your instruction as you're developing it and again each time you deliver it. One way to do the former is to ask an expert colleague (e.g., library media specialist, classroom teacher, reading specialist, technology coordinator) to review your lesson plan and give feedback; this can even be a way to begin a collaborative relationship.

A pilot test is another way to formatively evaluate instruction. A pilot test requires only a few students to experience the lesson and provide feedback. Or, you might choose to sit with one or two students as they work in a learning center or use a job aid, recording their comments and suggestions.

Have you ever taught the same lesson several times during a day or several times a week? Did you notice how much better your lesson became by the time you had taught it once or twice? It's probably because you made adjustments to the lesson each time you taught it, to make it more effective for the next time. Each time you taught your lesson, it served as a field test for the next time. Field tests are a third choice for conducting a formative evaluation of lessons.

A field test requires delivery of instruction in the actual learning setting to a real learning audience (similar to your target audience) and using the results to change the lesson for the next time you deliver it. Another way to conduct a field test is to ask someone else to deliver the instruction while you observe and take notes about what works and what needs improvement.

The most important source of information for a formative evaluation, whether formal or informal, is the learning audience—your students. By including students in the instructional-evaluation process, you learn valuable information about the lesson's effectiveness, and also make a statement about how you value student input. When appropriate, incorporate their suggestions into your instruction.

Collecting feedback from students can take place during a more informal discussion or focus group or, more formally, in written or electronic form. If it's a long lesson, consider collecting this information around midpoint in the lesson; otherwise, it is preferable to wait until the lesson is completed. For example, if teaching a full-day workshop to teachers, you may want to do an informal evaluation at the end of the morning session to leave time to make some changes during the lunch break. If teaching a unit (series of related lessons), you may choose to evaluate each lesson in the unit or evaluate about halfway through the unit in order to make needed modifications in the remaining lessons.

Figure 5.5 presents an example of a feedback exercise that can be used for individual class sessions. The student's name is made optional to allow anonymity. Sometimes students fear teachers will take offense at any negative information in their assessment. One way to approach this is to reassure students that you *need* their feedback because you want to make your instruction the best it can be. Occasionally, consider omitting the name line entirely to ensure that students will feel more comfortable in providing frank and honest comments. You can also end the exercise with an opportunity for students to address concerns or problems not covered by the other questions. This, too, is optional.

Figure 5.5. Feedback Exercise

Name (optional): _____

Date: _____

The purpose of this exercise is to give you an opportunity to reflect on today's class session and to maintain a dialogue with the instructor, allowing her to respond as well as to use your comments and suggestions as formative evaluation for course improvement. *Although it is required, it will not be evaluated as part of your course grade.*

Please answer every question.

1. What is the one thing you learned today that was most interesting to you?

2. What is one activity during today's session that you really liked?

3. What is one thing about today's class session that you would like to improve, correct, or change? Include any stress, concern, or unanswered question you have about the topic.

4. What is one skill you improved as a result of today's session and how might you apply it in practice in your field?

5. Do you have any unanswered questions about today's class session?

Additional comments (optional):

Outcome-Based Evaluation

If you are considering ways to measure the benefits to your target audience of the entire instructional program, outcome-based evaluation might be a viable option. Outcome-based evaluation, rooted in the philosophy of John Dewey, became popular (and caused quite a controversy) in the late twentieth century with its call for national reform of public education and the advent of the standards movement.

An outcome-based evaluation plan was developed to measure the success of *S.O.S. for Information Literacy* (http://www.informationliteracy.org). S.O.S. (Situation, Outcomes, Strategies) is a web-based, multimedia database of information literacy teaching ideas and lesson plans, created by Marilyn Arnone and Ruth Small at Syracuse University.

School librarians, classroom teachers, reading specialists, and other educators from around the world contribute their best lesson plans to the S.O.S. database. Teams of evaluators determine if each lesson plan meets the criteria for success, and, if not, the contributor is given specific, concrete suggestions for making the lesson "S.O.S. compliant."

Figure 5.6 is a small part of an outcome-based evaluation plan. Notice that the outcomes are expressed as program goals, and a plan for how data will be collected, from whom, when, and the criteria for success are specified for each indicator. The target audience is K–8 library media specialists and classroom teachers participating in building the S.O.S. database.

Whether using an outcome-based evaluation or some other method for evaluating the inquiry-skills instructional program, this type of information is critical for identifying the benefits of your program and conveying those benefits to administrators and the school board. In difficult economic times, evaluation is essential for survival.

Figure 5.6. Outcome Evaluation Plan

Outcome #1: *Participants (e.g., library media specialists and classroom teachers) will improve their information literacy skills (ILS) instruction.*

Indicator(s)	Given a minimum of six months exposure to SOS, 25 percent or greater (n=100) of participants will report perceived improvement of their IL skills instruction. (Results will be correlated with level of participation).
Data Source (Where data will be found)	1. Online questionnaire using *Likert-type scale* 2. Online focus group sessions
To Whom (Segment of population to which this indicator is applied)	A group of 100+ pilot users of SOS who have been invited to participate in the development cycle of the resource.
Data Intervals (Points at which information is collected)	1. 6-month intervals beginning in October of 2003 and continuing throughout the development phase (approximately two years). 2. January 2004, January 2005.
Target (the number, percent, variation or other measure of change)	25 percent or greater of the 100 pilot users will report perceived improvement in the first 6-month interval escalating to 50 percent or more by the end of the development cycle.

Web-Based Instructional Tools

Any discussion of teaching techniques would not be complete without considering technology integration and resources, Web 2.0 tools and services, and content-rich websites. We need to look at how we can use emerging technologies to support the thinking processes at each phase of the inquiry process, support differentiated learning, and create collaborative learning environments. When introduced at the appropriate phase of inquiry, technology tools can engage and motivate students, support higher-order thinking skills, and encourage interactive learning.

What Is Web 2.0?

Web 2.0 is an umbrella term for the second wave of the World Wide Web; it is loosely defined as the evolution to a more social, interactive web that gives everyone a chance to create, share, publish, and collaborate. The term refers to websites and applications that foster user participation, collaboration, interactivity, and content sharing. Web 2.0 includes wikis, blogs, photo and video sharing, social networking, tagging and bookmarking, online discussion boards, podcasts, and multiuser virtual environments and syndication. These tools allow ordinary users to post content online, making anyone with an Internet connection a participant and potential resource. Tim O'Reilly, who is credited with coining the term Web 2.0, wanted to denote the major changes in the web that were taking shape after the dot-com bust (O'Reilly, 2005). Before Web 2.0, webmasters or programmers posted Internet content and the exchange of information was mostly one way. Personal websites became blogs, text-based tutorials turned into streaming media, photos in desktop folders became organized collections being shared online, and taxonomy turned into folksonomy.

The following list summarizes the principal concepts underlying Web 2.0:

- *User participation:* Web 2.0 applications encourage users to share their ideas, opinions, content, and more. It facilitates and offers strong support for sharing through active participation. "A core concept of Web 2.0 is that people are the content of the site. That is, a site is not populated with information for users to consume. Instead services are provided to individual users for them to build their network of friends and other groups (professional, recreational, etc.). The content of a site then comprises user provided information that attracts new members of an ever-expanding network" (O'Reilly, 2005).

- *Harnessing collective intelligence:* Collective intelligence is defined in Wikipedia as "a shared or group intelligence that emerges from the collaboration and competition of many individuals." It is based on the web's original premise of shared information. Harnessing the collective intelligence of large groups of people in problem solving, writing, and other activities adds to the participants' experience. New applications, services, and tools have been developed to allow users to more directly share. Wikipedia, an online encyclopedia that anyone can add to or edit an entry, along with Delicious, a social bookmarking site, and Flickr, a photo-sharing tool, are a few of the pioneers of Web 2.0 services. Within schools, websites such as VoiceThread, Dipity, Wikispaces, and Edublogs encourage students to share their ideas and opinions.

- *Collaboration:* Free, flexible, and server-based programs are readily available for collaboration. Students can open their browsers and begin to edit word-processing documents or spreadsheets in Google Docs or Zoho Notebook, create mindmaps in Bubbl.Us or

Mindmeister, or organize, share, and swap information in Wikispaces and hold online meetings in Skype. Students no longer need to save a document and e-mail it to a classmate, edit it, and send it back. Today's electronic documents allow collaborators to work in a synchronous environment on a single document; groups of students can create, share, and edit them online. Students can connect with each other and explore how their interests and abilities can be used to enhance class projects.

Web 2.0 applications are changing how we, including our students, interact with each other and the world. In our day-to-day lives, we are initiating exchanges of text and multimedia information through new web tools that enable us to create, share, socialize, and collaborate with colleagues, family members, classmates, and newly developed network contacts. These same tools can motivate and engage students in the learning process.

Top 10 Reasons for Using Web 2.0 Tools in Education

1. Motivate and involve students in learning, using tools that many are already using for personal purposes.

2. Align with the American Association of School Librarians' (2007) *Standards for the 21st-Century Learner* and International Society for Technology in Education's (2007) *National Educational Technology Standards*.

3. Prepare students with authentic skills for working in the real world.

4. Encourage collaborative learning strategies.

5. Support learning as a social process.

6. Allow interactive learning.

7. Provide students with authentic audiences.

8. Offer free and fun use.

9. Provide an anytime, anywhere learning environment.

10. Connect students to a global community of learners.

Web 2.0 Technology and Inquiry

Most of the professional literature on pedagogy advises that to prepare our students best for the complex world in which they will live and work we need to develop interactive, inquiry based, technology-rich curricula. John Bransford and his colleagues in *How People Learn* argue that active, rather than passive, learners are better able to understand complex material and can more effectively transfer information and concepts learned in one setting to the process of solving problems encountered in another (Bransford, Brown, and Cocking, 2000). In other words, when students are actively engaged in their learning and are required to apply what they have learned, they retain that knowledge. Not surprisingly, research shows that today's digital students learn more when engaged in meaningful, relevant, and intellectually stimulating schoolwork and that the use of technology can increase the frequency of this type of learning (North Central Regional Educational Laboratory [NCREL] and the Metiri Group, 2003).

We know that technology can support more powerful knowledge-building experiences for learners "if we integrate well-designed technologies in the context of meaningful, mindful inquiry projects, non-presentational pedagogies, access to resources and tools, and adequate support for technological maintenance and pedagogical renewal" (Breuleux, 2001: 3). The I+M-PACT and ARCS models are just as applicable to instructional-media development as to overall lesson plan design. That is, you need to identify the purpose of your media or technology, who will use it, and what you know about them that is relevant to successful learning with your media, what content is appropriate for the selected medium, and what instructional techniques will be effective using this medium.

Active, engaged learning is one of the major benefits of integrating technology into the curriculum; however, knowledge of pedagogy and how people learn must drive decisions on which technology is best suited for specific learning needs. "Pouring a solid foundation of good pedagogical design before adding on the layer of technology can become a critical factor in the success rate of technology integration" (Ziegenfuss, 2005: 19).

In developing the *Standards for the 21st-Century Learner*, the American Association of School Librarians (AASL) (2007) identified nine common beliefs that support learning. The second belief listed, "Inquiry provides a framework for learning," focuses on students' developing not only the skills, but also the disposition to use the skills, along with an understanding of their own responsibilities and self-assessment strategies. The inquiry approach is focused on using and learning content as a means to develop information-processing and problem-solving skills. It's a student-centered approach, with the teacher as a facilitator of learning. Students are involved in the construction of knowledge through active involvement and, most important, asking questions; questions are at the heart of inquiry learning.

Today's digital information environment adds another layer of skills to those that are essential for inquiry-based learning. Technology and, in particular, Web 2.0 tools and services can be used throughout the inquiry process to support the appropriate thinking skills. The key is to focus on student learning, not the Web 2.0 technology. Use the phases of inquiry outlined in the Stripling Inquiry Model to help match the best technology tools to support the thinking processes and instructional strategies associated with the different inquiry phases. The result will be an increase in the effectiveness of both the learning experience and the use of technology. Table 5.1 outlines the inquiry phases aligned with digital literacy and inquiry skills, instructional strategies, and Web 2.0 technology tools.

A Sampling of Web 2.0 Tools

Now in its eighth year, The Horizon Report identifies and examines emerging technologies for their potential impact on and use in teaching, learning, and creative inquiry. *The 2010 Horizon Report K–12 Edition* noted the increased importance of technology in students' lives:

> Technology is increasingly a means for empowering students, a method for communication and socializing, and a ubiquitous, transparent part of their lives. Once seen as an isolating influence, technology is now recognized as a primary way to stay in touch and take control of one's own learning. Multisensory, ubiquitous, and interdisciplinary, technology is integrated into nearly everything we do. It gives students a public voice and a means to reach beyond the classroom for interaction and exploration. (Johnson et al., 2010: 4)

Realizing the importance of technology in teaching and learning, the American Association of School Librarians (2011) has taken a lead role in identifying Web 2.0 tools and services that support "inquiry-based teaching and learning" and "foster the qualities of innovation, creativity,

Table 5.1. Digital Literacy and Inquiry Skills

INQUIRY PHASE	DIGITAL LITERACY AND INQUIRY SKILLS	Teaching and Learning Strategies	Technology Tools/Resources
Connect	Focus • Central themes and big ideas	Conversing Facilitated conversation Small group discussion & dialogue	EduBlogs, Ning, Wikispaces, Skype
		Engagement and exploration activities	Google Earth, Teacher Tube, Flickr, WatchKnow, Museum Box
	Contextualization • Search terms/vocabulary	Pre-reading aids (visual organizers, structures overviews, semantic maps)	Mindmeister, Bubbl.us
	• Schema and cognitive maps	Research journals Learning logs	GoogleDocs, Zoho Suite
		Charting the inquiry/ information searching process	
		Webbing	
Wonder	Questioning • Provocative and diverse sources → higher-level questions	Class brainstorming	GoogleDocs templates, Edistorm
		Peer questioning	
		Question stems	Mindmeister, Bubbl.us
		Anticipation guide	Blogs
		Journals	
Investigate	Relational search strategies	Find information	Google Diigo Clusty Ask Kartoo Intute Twitter Google Reader
	Participatory organization • Tagging and personal organization of web information	Ideas from text/connections to prior knowledge	
	Sourcing • Evaluating digital sources for authority, purpose, currency, credibility, perspective		Google Docs, Zoho
	Corroboration • Accuracy	Evaluate information	
	Relational thinking • Comparing one source against another (point of view) • Commonalities and differences among multiple perspectives	Two-column note taking • Notes/reflection • Main idea/details, examples	Wikispaces (pathfinders) Jing, Jog the Web, LiveBinders
	Connected meaning • Linking ideas between texts	Charting, mindmapping Organize sources	Diigo, SimplyBox Netvibes, Pageflakes, 30 Boxes, Evernote
	Deep reading	Timelines	Dipity

(Continued)

Table 5.1. Digital Literacy and Inquiry Skills (continued)

INQUIRY PHASE	DIGITAL LITERACY AND INQUIRY SKILLS	Teaching and Learning Strategies	Technology Tools/Resources
Investigate (Continued)	Critical literacy skills: • Questioning the text • Reading for analysis • Evaluating information • Reading for implicit meaning Media literacy • "Read" and interpret information in multiple formats Danger of visuals as illustration only, "graphic seduction" Ethical participation Digital citizenship skills: • Determining authorship • Paraphrasing and citing • Differentiating between proprietary and creative commons information • Seeking alternative perspectives	Questioning: teacher-to-student, student-to-teacher, student-to-student Discussion Interview Guided practice Composing Use of rubric with specific criteria Select format based on needs of topic and audience Teacher and peer conferencing	Podcasting VoiceThread
Construct	Synthesis • Synthesize large amounts of specific bits of information Finding patterns and relationships • Finding relationships among ideas • Discovering new connections Developing own conclusions • Testing interpretations against evidence • Developing a line of argument with points and counterpoints/evidence	Charting, mindmapping Composing Questioning: teacher-to-student, student-to-teacher, student-to-student Discussion Timelines	Mindmeister, Bubbl.us, SpicyNodes Edublogs, Wikispaces, GoogleDocs, Zoho Suite Prezi Polleverywhere, GoogleDocs, Zoho Suite Edublogs, E-mail, Instant Messenger, Skype, Twitter Dipity
Express	Shared learning • Social tools Authenticity • Real-world applications Creative thinking • Create own messages	Select format based on needs of topic and audience Use of rubric with specific criteria Teacher and peer conferencing	Voicethread, Glogster, Jing, Splashcast, Podcast, Animoto, GoAnimate Google Docs, Zoho Suite Quick Response Codes (QR codes) Skype, Blogs
Reflect	Metacognition and self-assessment • Assessing both product and process	Feedback from teacher and peers Reflection log: I used to think/Now I know	EduBlogs, Wikispaces, E-mail GoogleDocs, VoiceThread, Podcast, Prezi

Skype, http://skype.com: Make free Internet calls, anywhere in the world. TIP: To engage and excite students in meaningful curriculum topics, invite experts into your classroom and have students develop thoughtful questions to interact and investigate.

Twitter, http://twitter.com: Share and discover what's happening right now through "tweets" of 140 characters. TIP: During the Connect inquiry phase, challenge social studies students to create "historical figures" from a period of history you are about to study via tweets of 140 characters.

Digital Storytelling

International Children's Digital Library, http://childrenslibrary.org: Share over 4,500 digital books in 54 languages from 228 countries with your students. TIP: Choose a richly illustrated book from another language and have your students write a story to align with the illustrations; translate the original story and compare the two.

Jing, http://techsmith.jing.com: Create a video tutorial by capturing anything that appears on your desktop while simultaneously adding a voice-over. TIP: Differentiate learning by creating video tutorials for your students.

Storybird, http://storybird.com: Create a digital story by reversing the process—start with images and unlock the story inside. TIP: Encourage student creativity through visual clues and collaboratively developing the story.

Web-Based Instructional Resources

In addition to Web 2.0 tools and services there are excellent, content-rich resources and references that motivate and engage students:

The Annenberg Learner, http://www.learner.org: A premier resource for arts, foreign language, mathematics, science, social studies, and language arts, this resource contains many formats—videos, interactive programs, and workshops—and distance learning can be searched by grade to find classroom and lesson ideas.

CK–12 Flexbooks, http://www.ck12.org/flexbook/: CK–12 Flexbooks plan to reduce the cost of textbooks for the K–12 market in the U.S. and worldwide. Using an open-content, web-based collaborative model termed the "FlexBook," CK–12 plans to lead the way in the distribution of high-quality educational content through online textbooks.

Digital Vaults, http://www.digitalvaults.org: Photos, documents, and popular media from the National Archives provide resources and interactive opportunities for users to access materials on endless U.S. historical topics and themes. The user can then organize the resources in any number of ways to relate our country's history and tell a story. There are options to create unique posters, movies, and pathway challenges and maintain individualized online collections.

Edsitement, http://edsitement.neh.gov: Check out this site for great educational material, suggested websites, and lesson plans in literature/language arts, art/culture, social studies/history, and foreign language.

Edutopia, http://www.edutopia.org: Through the Edutopia.org website, the George Lucas Educational Foundation spreads the word about ideal, interactive learning environments to enable others to adapt these successes locally. Search by keyword from more than 2,200 features on this site or browse a collection of more than 100 downloadable videos to find the tools needed to help in promoting an interactive learning environment. Check their weekly newsletter for new ideas and resources.

EduWeb, http://www.eduweb.com: Grounded in the idea of game-based learning, students work through creative learning games and activities, all the while learning in a fun and engaging environment. Challenge students to find cool activities for learning.

Exploratorium, http://www.exploratorium.edu: Dive into a unique exploration of science, art, and human perception in online extension of the Exploratorium Museum. Watch, view, experience, learn, and play using hundreds of webpages and activities. Take a gross-out walk, dissect a cow's eye, make your own petroglyph . . . the choices are endless.

Field Trip Earth, http://www.fieldtripearth.org/index.xml: Field Trip Earth can take the sting out of economic hard times. Field Trip Earth is the inexpensive way to take a virtual field trip. This website monitors wildlife preservation projects all over the world and your class can go, too. What's best is that you never have to leave the classroom! Includes interviews with field researchers.

GeoCube, http://www.geo-cube.eu: Based on the principle of the Rubik Cube with six faces and 54 topics, Geocube calls itself the world of geography at your fingertips. Move the Geocube around with your mouse and explore the faces and topics as you learn about geography in a fun, engaging way.

Global School, http://www.globalschoolnet.org: One of the oldest and most reliable sites on the web, Global School creates opportunities for teachers and students around the world to work together on international-based projects. Join them for webinars or a cyberfair.

International Children's Digital Library, http://en.childrenslibrary.org: The largest digital collection of children's books, ICDL contains over 4,400 books in 54 languages representing 64 countries with applications for the iPhone and the iPad.

The Jason Project, http://www.jason.org/public/whatis/start.aspx: Connect your students with great explorers and great events in science with The Jason Project. It offers free online curriculum designed primarily for the middle grades but can be adapted to fit any grade level.

Khan Academy, http://www.khanacademy.org: This popular, highly regarded video library provides thousands of videos with alternative, engaging instruction in math, science, finance, and history. Constantly expanding and improving, this is a rich resource for instruction and learning.

Library of Congress, http://www.loc.gov/index.html: The Library of Congress website has over 13 million digitized primary-source items. Your first stop in this content-rich resource needs to be the American Memory Project to browse 100 separate collections arranged by topic. Teachers, students, parents, and the community can all find something here.

Lingt Language, http://lingtlanguage.com: Get your students speaking in another language, interacting with assignments, and responding. Lingt Language allows students to practice their foreign language skills online by allowing teachers to build assignments online that use voice, video, images, and text with the Lingt online editor.

MIT Open Courseware, http://ocw.mit.edu/high-school/: Don't miss this resource created by MIT for high schools to have open courseware materials for biology, calculus, and physics. High school teachers can use these materials to further enhance the education of their students in the classroom. It includes labs and video demonstrations.

NASA, http://www.nasa.gov/audience/forstudents/index.html: Space, the final frontier. Enhance the study of science and technology by employing the diverse resources available from NASA, including video clips, podcasts, NASA television, live space station video, and blogs. Be sure to check out NASA Kids Club for new learning games.

National Archives' Digital Classroom, http://www.archives.gov/education/: The National Archives' Digital Classroom offers a multitude of resources for the use of primary sources in the classroom. With access to copies of primary documents from the holdings of the National Archives of the United States, teachers can develop their own activities and lesson plans that make historical periods come alive for their students or choose from dozens of resources that have already been developed and are featured.

National Geographic, http://www.nationalgeographic.com: This well-known print magazine is online and covers a huge range of subjects, from space and the environment to animals and even world music (where you can listen to thousands of artists).

National Science Digital Library, http://nsdl.org: The National Science Digital Library includes a variety of educational resources to further STEM (science, technology, engineering, and mathematics) education. Browse the science literacy maps, short science refreshers, free multimedia downloads, or subject-area collections to find just what you need to enhance student learning.

Our Documents, http://www.ourdocuments.gov/index.php?flash=true&/: American history can come alive with resources from Our Documents. One hundred important documents from American history are featured on this site, along with specialized tools for enhancing the study of them. Search the Teacher Sourcebook for lesson plans.

PBS Teachers, http://www.pbs.org/teachers/: PBS, a leader in programming, offers standards-based resources in the arts, health and fitness, mathematics, reading/language arts, science/technology, and social studies on this site. It contains lesson plans, activities, and other materials that are tied to PBS programming, both on-air and online.

Read, Write, Think, http://www.readwritethink.org: Created by teachers for teachers to offer the best materials for reading and language arts education. The site focuses on learning language, learning through language, and learning about language. Great site for any language arts, ESL, or English teacher.

Smithsonian Education, http://smithsonianeducation.org: A content-rich website for families, students, and educators, the Smithsonian Education website offers browsable lesson plans (searchable by subject, keyword, or grade level), IdeaLabs, student interactive tutorials that enhance the use of the site, and much more.

S.O.S. for Information Literacy, http://informationliteracy.org: S.O.S. for Information Literacy is a dynamic, collaborative, web-based multimedia resource for educators, K to 16, that will help you to effectively incorporate information literacy into your lesson plans. This site links lesson plans and teaching ideas for information literacy through a comprehensive quality-control system to ensure that lessons are high caliber.

TED, http://www.ted.com: TED is a remarkable website sharing ideas from the world's most innovative thinkers and experts related to technology, entertainment, design, business, science, and global issues. Watch, listen to, learn, discuss, and spread TED.

Thinkfinity, http://www.thinkfinity.org: Thinkfinity offers thousands of lesson plans and interactives that align to both state and national standards. They have a consortium that includes partners National Geographic Xpeditions, Smithsonian's History Explorer, Arts Edge, and other leaders in the education field. Easily search for materials by keyword, subject, grade level, or type of resource.

Case Study #5: Harry and Sally Plan Instructional Strategies

At the end of the former planning meeting, Harry and Sally were clear on the content and standards they wanted to focus on in this unit; they now needed to decide what instructional strategies would be best. Through discussions with Sally, Harry was aware of the different academic levels represented in her class; this was going to be challenging for them. Harry began the meeting by discussing possible teaching strategies that would easily incorporate Web 2.0 tools for differentiated instruction and increased student engagement. He felt that for this research project he wanted to help students refine their inquiry questions and increase their understanding of how to organize and manage the information they were researching to make sense of it.

Harry and Sally discussed using a collaborative project-based approach where students are presented with a simulation of real-life experience: students receive a letter or e-mail informing them that they have been appointed ambassador to a specific country. Sally suggests that they work in teams and Harry agrees. The student team has 10 days to research the country and prepare their staff (the class) on what they need to know about the country. Harry suggests they introduce wikis to the students. Students could start using the wikis by posting what they already know and posing questions they have about their country; they will continue to use it throughout the project to share and organize the information they are finding. After Harry shows Sally a few examples of wikis used in this way, she agrees. They plan to discuss an evaluation rubric the next time they meet.

Extension Questions

1. Students in Sally's class have different academic abilities and technology skills. How would you provide extra support to students who might need it?

2. Harry plans to teach students how to use a wiki to support the "wonder" and "investigate" phases of inquiry. What other Web 2.0 tools might you suggest to Sally to support other phases of inquiry? How do they support the thinking skills needed at the phase of inquiry?

References

American Association of School Librarians (AASL). 2007. *Standards for the 21st-Century Learner*. Chicago: American Library Association. http://www.ala.org/ala/mgrps/divs/aasl/guidelinesandstandards/learningstandards/AASL_Learning_Standards_2007.pdf.

———. 2011. "Best Websites for Teaching and Learning." American Library Association. Accessed August 1. http://www.ala.org/ala/mgrps/divs/aasl/guidelinesandstandards/bestlist/bestwebsites.cfm.

Annetta, Len. 2007. "Virtually a New Way of Learning: Video Games and Simulations as Teaching Tools." *Multimedia and Internet in Schools* 6 (November/December): 9–13.

Arnone, Marilyn P., Ruth V. Small, and Barbara K. Stripling (Eds.). 2010. *From the Creative Minds of 21st Century Librarians.* Syracuse, NY: Syracuse University Center for Digital Literacy. http://digitalliteracy.syr.edu/data/From_The_Creative_Minds_Book.pdf.

Bandura, Albert. 1982. "Self-Efficacy Mechanism in Human Agency." *The American Psychologist* 37, no. 2: 122–147.

Barkley, Elizabeth F. 2009. *Student Engagement Techniques: A Handbook for College Faculty.* New York: Jossey-Bass. Kindle Edition (unpaginated).

Bransford, John D., Ann L. Brown, and Rodney R. Cocking (Eds.). 2000. *How People Learn: Brain, Mind, Experience, and School.* Washington, DC: National Academies Press.

Breuleux, Alain. 2001. "Imagining the Past, Interpreting the Possible, Cultivating the Future: Technology, and the Renewal of Teaching and Learning." *Education Canada* 41, no. 3 (Fall): 12–15.

Casteel, J. Doyle, and Robert J. Stahl. 1973. *The Social Science Observation Record: A Guide for Pre-service and In-service Teachers Participating in Microteaching.* Gainesville, FL: P. K. Yonge Lab, Florida State University.

Csikszentmihalyi, Mihalyi. 1990. *Flow, the Psychology of Optimal Experience.* New York: Harper & Row.

International Society for Technology in Education. 2007. *National Educational Technology Standards: Students.* ISTE. http://www.iste.org/standards/nets-for-students/nets-student-standards-2007.aspx.

Johnson, L., R. Smith, A. Levine, and K. Haywood. 2010. *The 2010 Horizon Report: K–12 Edition.* Austin, TX: The New Media Consortium.

Lenhart, Amanda, Joseph Kahne, Ellen Middaugh, Alexandra Macgill, Chris Evans, and Jessica Vitak. 2008. *Teens, Video Games and Civics: Summary of Findings.* Pew Internet & American Life Project, Pew Research Center. http://pewinternet.org/Reports/2008/Teens-Video-Games-and-Civics/01-Summary-of-Findings/Summary-of-Findings.aspx.

Levin, Tama, and Ruth Long. 1981. *Effective Instruction.* Alexandria, VA: ASCD.

Marzano, Robert J., Debra J. Pickering, and Jane E. Pollock. 2001. *Classroom Instruction That Works: Research-Based Strategies for Increasing Student Achievement.* Alexandria, VA: Association for Supervision and Curriculum Development.

Masie, Elliott. 2011. "QuickTalks: Elliott Masie: Gaming, Simulation, and Virtualization." SkillsoftTV: Video Resources for Learning Professionals. Accessed August 1. http://bit.ly/pLAVoS/.

North Central Regional Educational Laboratory (NCREL) and the Metiri Group. 2003. *enGauge©21st Century Skills: Literacy in the Digital Age.* Naperville, IL; Los Angeles, CA: NCREL and Metiri Group.

O'Reilly, Tim. 2005. "What Is Web 2.0?" O'Reilly, September 30. http://oreilly.com/web2/archive/what-is-web-20.html.

Prensky, Marc. 2001. *Digital Natives, Digital Immigrants.* Marc Prensky. http://www.marcprensky.com/writing/prensky%20-%20digital%20natives,%20digital%20immigrants%20-%20part1.pdf.

Project Tomorrow. 2010. *Creating Our Future: Students Speak Up about their Vision for 21st Century Learning.* Irvine, CA: Project Tomorrow. http://www.tomorrow.org/speakup/pdfs/SU09NationalFindingsStudents&Parents.pdf.

Rossett, Allison, and Jeannette H. Gautier-Downes. 1991. *A Handbook of Job Aids.* San Diego, CA: Pfeiffer Associates.

Rowe, Mary Budd. 1987. "Wait Time: Slowing Down May Be a Way of Speeding Up." *American Educator* 11 (Spring): 38–43, 47.

Rowe, Mary Budd 1996. "Science, Silence, and Sanctions." *Science and Children* (September): 35–37. http://web.missouri.edu/~hanuscind/sciencesilencesanctions.pdf.

Shaftel, Fannie, and George Shaftel. 1967. *Role-Playing for Social Values*. Englewood Cliffs, NJ: Prentice-Hall.

Small, R.V. 1999. "An Exploration of Motivational Strategies Used by Library Media Specialists during Library and Information Skills Instruction." *School Library Media Research* 2 (January). http://www.ala.org/ala/mgrps/divs/aasl/aaslpubsandjournals/slmrb/slmrcontents/volume21999/vol2small.cfm.

Small, R. V., B. M. Dodge, and X. Jiang. 1996. "Student Perceptions of Boring and Interesting Instruction." *Proceedings of the Annual Conference of the Association for Educational Communications and Technology*, Indianapolis.

Svinicki, Marilla D., and Nancy M. Dixon. 1987. "The Kolb Model Modified for Classroom Activities." *College Teaching* 35, no. 4: 141–146.

Tilaro, Angie, and Allison Rossett. 1993. "Creating Motivating Job Aids." *Performance & Instruction* 32, no. 9 (October): 13–19.

Tobin, Kenneth. 1987. "The Role of Wait Time in Higher Cognitive Level Learning." *Review of Educational Research* 57, no. 1 (Spring): 69–95.

VanGundy, A. B. 1988. *Techniques of Structured Problem-Solving*, 2nd ed. New York: Van Nostrand Reinhold.

Wright, Van O. 1989. "How to Use (Not Abuse) Role Plays." *Performance & Instruction* 28, no. 5 (May/June): 16–21.

Ziegenfuss, Donna. 2005. "By Instructional Design: Facilitating Effective Teaching and Learning with Technology." In *Integrating Technology in Higher Educations*, edited by M. O. Thirunarayanan and Aixa Perez-Prado. Lanham, MD: University Press of America.

DIGGING DEEPER

Bellanca, James, and Ron Brandt. 2010. *21st Century Skills: Rethinking How Students Learn*. Bloomington, IN: Solution Tree Press.

Berger, Pam. 2010. "Student Inquiry and Web 2.0." *School Library Monthly* 26, no. 5: 14–17.

Berger, Pam, and Sally Trexler. 2010. *Choosing Web 2.0 Tools for Teaching and Learning in a Digital World*. Santa Barbara, CA: Libraries Unlimited.

Burke, Kay. 2010. *Balanced Assessment: From Formative to Summative*. Bloomington, IN: Solution Tree Press.

Cash, Richard M. 2011. *Advancing Differentiation: Thinking and Learning for the 21st Century*. Minneapolis, MN: Free Spirit Publishing.

Gregory, Gayle. 2008. *Differentiated Instructional Strategies in Practice: Training, Implementation, and Supervision*. Thousand Oaks, CA: Corwin Press.

Marzano, Robert J., Debra J. Pickering, and Tammy Heflebower. 2011. *The Highly Engaged Classroom*. Englewood, CO: Marzano Research Laboratory.

Popham, W. James. 2011. *Transformative Assessment in Action: An Inside Look at Applying the Process*. Alexandria, VA: ASCD.

Small, Ruth V., and Marilyn P. Arnone. 2000. *Turning Kids on to Research: The Power of Motivation*. Englewood, CO: Libraries Unlimited.

Stripling, Barbara K. 2003. "Inquiry-Based Learning." In *Curriculum Connections Through the Library*, edited by Barbara K. Stripling and Sandra Hughes-Hassell, 3–39. Westport, CT: Libraries Unlimited.

Tomlinson, Carol Ann, Kay Brimijoin, and Lane Narvaez. (2008). *The Differentiated School: Making Revolutionary Changes in Teaching and Learning*. Alexandria, VA: ASCD.

Zmuda, Allison. 2008. *Librarians as Learning Specialists: Meeting the Learning Imperative for the 21st Century*. Englewood, CO: Libraries Unlimited.

Bringing It All Together

School librarians are often called to leadership in the school, district, and profession. Through the critical roles of teacher and instructional partner, librarians can demonstrate leadership to both students and teachers, particularly in the essential twenty-first-century areas of digital and information literacy skills, technology fluency, and information ethics.

This book is intended to reinforce your skills as a library leader through a framework of instructional design called I+M-PACT (Inquiry + Motivation—Purpose, Audience, Content, Technique). This framework considers both learning and motivation in teaching for inquiry, ensuring that students will not only learn essential skills and concepts but do so in ways that are engaging and develop a lifelong thirst for knowledge.

This vital connection among learning, motivation, and inquiry is supported by research in our field. For example, in recent research on the impact of New York's school libraries on student achievement and motivation, Ruth Small and her research team found that librarians consider motivation and learning as inextricably linked (Small, Snyder, and Parker, 2009). One elementary principal's description of a lesson on Boolean operators by his school librarian demonstrates this:

> Last year [she] did something very interesting. She did a series of lessons on Boolean operators, and she just taught that every way possible. She did this great lesson—you know, candy bars and it's chocolate AND nuts!...Boy, the kids, you know, they will never forget...(Small, Shanahan, and Stasak, 2010).

The ways in which you choose to interpret and implement the I+M-PACT framework, in order to have an *impact* on those you serve, will be unique and individual to you, based on the culture of your school and the needs of your teachers and students.

In this final chapter, we provide a brief list of the key concepts from each of the first five chapters followed by selected assessment items related to that chapter's outcomes and indicators, which allow reflection on knowledge gained. You will notice that we also identify the level of Bloom's Taxonomy for each assessment item and its related chapter, in case you wish to go back and review a topic in more detail. We conclude this chapter and this book with some final thoughts about the importance of motivating student inquiry.

Our goal is to enable you to move from reflection to action. When considering the concepts in this book, decide how to apply them to your situation. By transforming the ideas into daily actions, you will be building a schoolwide culture of inquiry and motivation through your library program. You will empower your students and teachers to be engaged, twenty-first-century learners.

Assessing Your Learning

Chapter 1. Inquiry + Motivation Leads to Deep Understanding

Key Concepts

Teaching for understanding; inquiry, inquiry-related learning theories; the Stripling Model of Inquiry; extrinsic and intrinsic motivation; motivation theories; the ARCS Model of Motivational Design; dispositions; inquiry and motivation; the I+M-PACT Model; constructivist learning and teaching; designing motivating inquiry-based learning environments.

Reflection Activities

1. Name the six phases of Stripling's inquiry process. (Remembering)
2. Create at least one motivational strategy to address each of the four major elements of the ARCS Model of Motivational Design for inquiry-based learning for a lesson you are planning. (Creating)
3. Generate at least one constructivist teaching strategy that aligns with each phase of the inquiry process for your lesson. (Creating)

Chapter 2. Purpose: Beginning at the End

Key Concepts

Needs assessment; Bloom's Taxonomy; standards, indicators, and assessments; backward design; outcome-based evaluation; collaboration; the Motivation Overlay to Instruction; motivational goals; motivation and standards; motivational assessment; barriers to learning success.

Reflection Activities

1. Characterize the activities you would include in your lesson to conduct an instructional needs assessment for teaching inquiry learning in your library. (Analyzing)
2. Describe at least two ways you might assess learning outcomes and indicators in your inquiry-based lesson. (Applying)
3. Describe how time and scheduling constraints can become obstacles to inquiry learning success. (Applying)

Chapter 3. Students as Learning Audience

Key Concepts

Learning audience analysis; individual differences; cognitive styles; learning styles; Kolb's Learning Style Inventory; needs and attitudes; motivational profile; curiosity; relevance; confidence; perceived competence; learning responsibility; environmental factors.

Reflection Activities

1. Identify at least three important characteristics of your learning audience. (Applying)
2. Choose the most appropriate AASL Standards and Indicators for your learning audience's profile. (Evaluating)

3. Design a strategy for maximizing the environmental factors that support learning success and a strategy for minimizing environmental factors that inhibit learning success in your library. (Creating)

Chapter 4. Selecting and Organizing Content

Key Concepts

Curriculum and instruction alignment; information needs; information types; student needs, information types and inquiry; information quality, amount, scope, form, and design; introductory hook; direct instruction; modeling and guided practice; independent practice; sharing and reflection; learning assessment.

Reflection Activities

1. Explain the purpose and use for each of the three types of information elements. (Understanding)
2. Create a concept map or perform a task analysis for organizing or sequencing the content of your lesson. (Analyzing)
3. Provide an example of how each of the three guiding principles for Universal Design for Learning (UDL) might be applied when teaching for inquiry in your library. (Applying)

Chapter 5. Technique for Inquiry Teaching and Learning

Key Concepts

Differentiation of instruction; instructional methods; questioning; practice; discussion; brainstorming; role-playing; gaming; lecture; learning-support materials and activities; handouts; learning centers; job aids; learning styles; formative evaluation; outcome-based evaluation; Web 2.0; user participation; collective intelligence; collaboration; Web 2.0 tools that support inquiry.

Reflection Activities

1. Explain three ways you might differentiate instruction for motivating inquiry learning in your library. (Comprehending)
2. Compare digital literacy and inquiry skills with more traditional, print-based information skills. (Analyzing)
3. Identify at least one Web 2.0 tool that could be used to support each phase of the inquiry learning process. (Applying)
4. Create an evaluation plan you might use to assess inquiry learning and motivation for a specific group of students in your library. (Creating)

Final Thoughts

The path to effective instruction in the library is complex. You can motivate and empower your students to pursue inquiry by addressing the critical components of the I+M-PACT model of instructional design: Inquiry + Motivation—Purpose, Audience, Content, and Technique. You will become as excited about learning and inquiry as your students. There is no perfect lesson or perfect plan for teaching inquiry, but you will know that you're getting it right when one of your students races into the library during her lunch hour to find out what those "little white things" are that ants are dragging across the sidewalk, finds the answer on her own, and charges back to the playground to inform all her friends. That kind of motivation to inquire will last a lifetime.

References

Small, Ruth V., Kathryn A. Shanahan, and Megan Stasak. 2010. "The Impact of New York's School Libraries on Student Achievement and Motivation: Phase III." *School Library Media Research* 13 (April). American Library Association. http://www.ala.org/ala/mgrps/divs/aasl/aaslpubsandjournals/slmrb/slmrcontents/volume13/small_phase3.cfm.

Small, Ruth V., Jaime Snyder, and Katie Parker. 2009. "The Impact of New York's School Libraries on Student Achievement and Motivation: Phase I." *School Library Media Research* 12 (June). American Library Association. http://www.ala.org/ala/mgrps/divs/aasl/aaslpubsandjournals/slmrb/slmrcontents/volume12/small_phase2.cfm.

Perceived Competence in Information Skills Scale

Perceived Competence in Information Skills

HOW CONFIDENT ARE YOU?

DIRECTIONS: This is NOT a test. Your school librarian is interested in knowing how CONFIDENT you feel about a number of research activities. Please give your honest response about how confident you are. The information you provide will help your school librarian and/or classroom teacher plan instruction that focuses on your needs as a learner. *Read each statement carefully. Then, circle the response that represents how true the statement is for you.*

1. DEVELOPING MY RESEARCH QUESTIONS AND TOPICS

I am CONFIDENT in my ability to:

	Not at all true	Usually not true	Sometimes true	Usually true	Very true
–Formulate *smaller* (more specific) questions that help me narrow down my big (broad) research topic.	◯	◯	◯	◯	◯
–Know when a topic is *too broad* or *too narrow* for a research paper.	◯	◯	◯	◯	◯
–Understand the relationship of one concept (e.g., solar system) to another (e.g., planets).	◯	◯	◯	◯	◯

2. IDENTIFYING SOURCES OF INFORMATION

I am CONFIDENT in my ability to:

	Not at all true	Usually not true	Sometimes true	Usually true	Very true
–Identify a good starting point for researching a topic I don't know much about.	◯	◯	◯	◯	◯
–Choose the best sources of information for my particular research topic.	◯	◯	◯	◯	◯
–Tell the difference between a primary and a secondary resource.	◯	◯	◯	◯	◯

(Continued)

Perceived Competence in Information Skills (*Continued*)

3. FINDING AND USING INFORMATION

I am CONFIDENT in my ability to:

	Not at all true	Usually not true	Sometimes true	Usually true	Very true
–Locate information on my research topic in sources like books, databases, encyclopedias, and websites.	○	○	○	○	○
–Understand the meaning of terms like keyword, bibliography, and footnote.	○	○	○	○	○
–Locate information inside a source once I find it, such as using the index, table of contents, etc.	○	○	○	○	○
–Determine whether the information I find is appropriate for my information need.	○	○	○	○	○
–Use technology tools to help organize new information I find.	○	○	○	○	○

4. EVALUATING THE SOURCES OF INFORMATION I FIND

I am CONFIDENT in my ability to:

	Not at all true	Usually not true	Sometimes true	Usually true	Very true
–Evaluate the truth of information that I find in books, websites, magazines, and in media.	○	○	○	○	○
–Know when it is important that information be up-to-date.	○	○	○	○	○
–Recognize if information I find is biased or slanted toward a particular point of view.	○	○	○	○	○

4. USING INFORMATION RESPONSIBLY

I am CONFIDENT in my ability to:

	Not at all true	Usually not true	Sometimes true	Usually true	Very true
–Give proper credit for sources I use when preparing a bibliography for a research paper.	○	○	○	○	○
–Write a research paper in my own words, adding my own ideas to new things I learn.	○	○	○	○	○
–Know when it is appropriate to use images created by someone else on my website.	○	○	○	○	○

Source: Arnone, M. P., R. V. Small, and R. Reynolds. 2010. "Supporting Inquiry by Identifying Gaps in Student Confidence: Development of a Measure of Perceived Competence." *School Libraries Worldwide* 16, no. 1: 55–70.

Lesson Planning Template

Appendix 2

Lesson Planning Template

GENERAL INFORMATION

Librarian:

Lesson Plan/Unit Title:

Appropriate Grade Level(s):   **Required Time:**

Library Context: (Check one below)

☐ Fixed   ☐ Flexible   ☐ Combination   ☐ Individualized Instruction

☐ Stand-alone lesson   ☐ Lesson in a unit   ☐ Multiple lessons in a unit

Collaboration Potential: ☐ None   ☐ Limited   ☐ Moderate   ☐ Intensive

Overview:

Current Topic(s):

Connection to State or Local Content Standards:

(Continued)

129

Lesson Planning Template *(Continued)*

AASL *Standards for the 21st-Century Learner* Goals: (Use as many as needed)

Standard/Indicator:

Benchmark for my students, if appropriate:

Standard/Indicator:

Benchmark for my students, if appropriate:

Standard/Indicator:

Benchmark for my students, if appropriate:

Standard/Indicator:

Benchmark for my students, if appropriate:

Standard/Indicator:

Benchmark for my students, if appropriate:

Standard/Indicator:

Benchmark for my students, if appropriate:

(Continued)

Lesson Planning Template *(Continued)*

Motivational Goals:

Assessment Methods and Criteria:

Required Resources and Materials:

NOTES (OPTIONAL)

Learner Profile (e.g., # of students, special needs, reading levels, etc.):

Incoming Motivation Levels (Select all that apply):

Attention: ☐ Low ☐ Medium ☐ High *(Add notes below)*

Relevance: ☐ Low ☐ Medium ☐ High

Confidence: ☐ Low ☐ Medium ☐ High

Satisfaction: ☐ Low ☐ Medium ☐ High

(Continued)

Lesson Planning Template *(Continued)*

INSTRUCTION AND ACTIVITIES: SESSION 1

Setup/Preparation:

Direct Instruction:

Modeling and Guided Practice:

Independent Practice:

Sharing and Reflecting:

(Continued)

Lesson Planning Template *(Continued)*

INSTRUCTION AND ACTIVITIES: SESSION ☐ *(Indicate session number)*

Setup/Preparation:

Direct Instruction:

Modeling and Guided Practice:

Independent Practice:

Sharing and Reflecting:

(Continued)

Lesson Planning Template *(Continued)*

INSTRUCTION AND ACTIVITIES: SESSION ☐ *(Indicate session number)*

Setup/Preparation:

Direct Instruction:

Modeling and Guided Practice:

Independent Practice:

Sharing and Reflecting:

(Continued)

Lesson Planning Template *(Continued)*

INSTRUCTION AND ACTIVITIES: SESSION ☐ *(Indicate session number)*

Setup/Preparation:

Direct Instruction:

Modeling and Guided Practice:

Independent Practice:

Sharing and Reflecting:

(Continued)

Tipping the Scales
Worksheet

Index

Page numbers followed by the letter "f" indicate figures; those followed by the letter "t" indicate tables.

New York City Inquiry Benchmark Skills, 73t–74t
reflective questions for inquiry cycle, 15t
Constructivist learning theory
  digital literacy and inquiry skills, 114t, 125
  inquiry phases, motivation strategies, and ARCS
    components, 56t
Content
  assessment of student learning, 88–89
  case study, 89
  content collaboration websites, 115–116
  curriculum and, 2–3, 22, 62–64, 124–125
  digital literacy and inquiry skills, 114t
  I+M-PACT Model, 11–12, 124–126
  independent practice, 87–88
  organizing, 84–88, 86f, 87f
  performance matrix, 26, 27t
  selecting and organizing, 124
  sharing and reflection, 88
  skills and, 26, 81–84
Co-planning, 31–35
Costa, Art, 10
Criteria, lesson planning, 31–35
Csikszentmihalyi, Mihalyi, 102
Cunningham, Donald J., 13, 16
Curiosity, 51
Curriculum
  alignment, 62–64, 75t–78t
  context, inquiry and motivation, 2–3, 22, 51, 61
  library instruction, 22–23, 61–62, 124–125

D

Day, Hi I., 51
Deci, Ed, 7–10
Delicious (website), 110
Demonstrations, 7, 24, 49, 65, 82, 91
  techniques, 97–98, 106
Designing inquiry-based learning
  backward, 24, 25f, 25t, 26, 30–31, 124
  constructivist, 2, 12–13, 17t, 56t, 124
  digital literacy and inquiry skills, 114t, 125
  environments, 2, 14, 16, 55–56
  information form and design, 83–84
  New York City Inquiry Benchmark Skills, 71,
    72t–74t
  outcome-based evaluation, 30–31, 109, 109f
Dewey, John, 4, 6, 12, 109
Dewey Decimal System
  in information seeking, 69
  literacy skills and, 73t, 76t, 77t
  mnemonics, 80
  practice activity, 97
  in skills assessment, 89, 94

Diagnostic, 13, 93–94
Dialogue, 99, 108f, 113t
Diary of Anne Frank (Frank), 102
Differentiating instruction, 91, 92–94
Digging deeper (resources), 20, 42, 59, 90, 122
Digital literacy and inquiry skills, 113t–114t,
    115–119, 125
Digital Vaults (website), 117
Diigo (website), 113t, 115
Dipity (website), 110, 113t–114t, 116
Direct instruction, 85–87
Discussion, strategies, 97–98
Dispositions, 9–10, 52
Dixon, Nancy M., 106
Dodge, Bernie, 49, 51, 103
Duffy, Thomas M., 13, 16
Dunn, Rita, 55

E

E-mail, 114t
E-V theory (expectancy-value theory), 8, 9
Edistorm (website), 98, 113t, 115
Edmodo (website), 98, 116
Edsitement (website), 116
Edublogs (website), 98, 110, 113t–114t, 116
Edutopia (website), 117
EduWeb (website), 118
Emotional environment for learning, self-
    assessment rubric, 8, 16t–17t
Engagement
  in constructivist learning, 12–13
  and enriching elements, 78
  and instructional/learning strategies, 103, 113t,
    120
  and learning environments, 54–55
  and Standards for the 21st-Century Learner, 37–38
  student, 4, 49, 91, 97
Enriched information elements, 65–66, 78–80
Environment, conducive to learning, 16t–17t
Environmental aspects of teaching, 16, 55–56
Evaluations
  formative, 107–108, 108f
  outcome-based, 109, 109f, 124
  testing, 107
Evernote (website), 103, 113t, 115
Expectations, 52
Express, inquiry phase, 5, 70
  digital literacy and inquiry skills, 114t
  and motivation strategies with ARCS
    components, 56t
  New York City Inquiry Benchmark Skills, 74t
  reflective questions for inquiry cycle, 15t

W

WatchKnow (website), 113t
Web 2.0
    applications in lectures, 103
    concepts, 125
    defined, 110
    reasons for using, 111–112
    resource sampling, 117–119
    social networking, 98
    tools/resources, 91–92, 110–112, 113t–114t,
        115–120
Web-based instruction
    case study, 120
    digital literacy and inquiry skills, 113t–114t, 125
    instructional materials, 110–112, 120, 113t–114t
    QR (Quick Response) Codes, 105–106, 105f, 114t
    resources, 117–120
    tools, 110–112, 113t–117t
Websites
    content collaboration, 115–116
    digital storytelling, 117
    instruction resources, web-based, 117–120
    lesson, 68
    manage and organize, 115, 125
    media sharing, 116
    QR (Quick Response) Codes, 105–106, 105f, 114t
    social network, 116–117

Weil, M., 79
Weiner, Bernard, 52
White, Gwynn, 26
Wiggins, Grant, 30
Wikipedia (website), 110
Wikispaces (website), 98, 104, 110–111, 113t–114t,
    116
Witkin, Herman A., 46–47
Wlodkowski, Raymond, 48
Wonder, inquiry phase, 5, 67
    digital literacy and inquiry skills, 113t
    and motivation strategies with ARCS
        components, 56t
    New York City Inquiry Benchmark Skills, 72t
    reflective questions for inquiry cycle, 15t
World Wide Web, 110
Wordle (website), 103, 116
Wright, Van O., 100f
Writing standards, 75t–78t

Z

Ziegenfuss, Donna, 112
Zoho (website)
    Notebook, 110
    Suite, 113t–114t
Zone of Proximal Development (ZPD) learning
    theory, 4

About the Authors

Ruth V. Small, PhD, is Laura J. & L. Douglas Meredith Professor and Director of the School Media Program in the School of Information Studies at Syracuse University (iSchool @ Syracuse). Her expertise is in the area of motivation, which she applies to a variety of information contexts, including inquiry teaching and learning in libraries. She has received two major national awards for her research in this area and has authored or co-authored more than 100 publications, including six books. Her current research focuses on the librarian's role in fostering children's creativity and innovative thinking; she shares some of her findings in this book. As founding director of Syracuse University's Center for Digital Literacy, Ruth has led or co-led more than 20 funded projects, including S.O.S. for Information Literacy, a multimedia database of lesson plans and teaching ideas, PLUS: Preparing Librarians for Urban Schools, a program for pre-service librarians committed to working in high-needs school libraries, and Project ENABLE: Expanding Nondiscriminatory Access By Librarians Everywhere, a project to train school librarians on ways to design and implement effective programs, resources, and services for students with disabilities. She has 12 years of experience as a K–12 classroom teacher and school librarian.

Marilyn P. Arnone, PhD, is a Research Associate Professor in the iSchool @ Syracuse, teaches in the school media program, and serves as co-director for Syracuse University's Center for Digital Literacy. Marilyn earned her doctorate in instructional design, development, and evaluation. Her recent research has explored perceived and actual competence in middle school children's information and digital literacies and considered various dispositions for learning with a special interest in curiosity and motivation for learning. She has authored or co-authored numerous publications including a book titled *Motivational Design: The Secret to Producing Effective Children's Media* (2005) and a series of *Curious Kids* storybooks with educator guides for introducing research skills to children in grades 1–3. She recently edited *From the Creative Minds of 21st-Century Librarians* with Ruth V. Small and Barbara K. Stripling, a free downloadable e-book published by the Center for Digital Literacy (http://digital-literacy .syr.edu). She is creator of *Curiosity Creek*, an online site for children in which older children create stories and materials for their younger counterparts in Pre-K to Grade 3. The mission of *Curiosity Creek* is to stimulate inquiry, imagination, and inventive thinking in the context of environmental science.

Barbara K. Stripling, DPS, has had a 30-year career as a classroom teacher, a school library media specialist, a library grant program director, a school district director of libraries and instructional services, and director of library programs at New Visions for Public Schools, a local education fund in New York City. She is currently Director of Library Services for the New York City Department of Education and recently completed her Doctorate of Professional Studies at Syracuse University. She is the creator of the Stripling Model of Inquiry, which has been adopted by the Library of Congress for its Teaching with Primary Sources initiative. Stripling has written or edited numerous books and articles, including her latest book, *Curriculum Connections Through the Library: Principles and Practice* (Libraries Unlimited, 2003), co-edited with Sandra Hughes-Hassell. She is a former president of the American Association of School Librarians and a former member of the American Library Association Executive Board. She recently completed her degree in the executive doctorate program in the iSchool @ Syracuse, researching the effect of teaching with primary sources on the development of historical empathy.

Pam Berger, CAS, is Director, Southern Westchester BOCES school library system, an educational technology/library consultant and trainer with more than 20 years of library experience, and adjunct faculty at the iSchool @ Syracuse. She is also publisher and editor of *Information Searcher*, the longest published newsletter in K–12 education designed specifically for professionals working to integrate technology into the curriculum and the library program. Her most recent book is *Choosing Web 2.0 Tools for Learning and Teaching in a Digital World* (2010). Pam has a Certificate of Advanced Study in School Administration from the College of New Rochelle.